WA ... .
ADJUSTMENT & REPAIR

A Practical Handbook on Modern Watches

BY

F. J. CAMM

Editor of
"Practical Mechanics" and "Practical Engineering"

WITH 151 ILLUSTRATIONS

British Library Cataloguing-in-Publication Data
A catalogue record for this book is available from the
British Library

A History of Clocks and Watches

Horology (from the Latin, Horologium) is the science of measuring time. Clocks, watches, clockwork, sundials, clepsydras, timers, time recorders, marine chronometers and atomic clocks are all examples of instruments used to measure time. In current usage, horology refers mainly to the study of mechanical timekeeping devices, whilst chronometry more broadly included electronic devices that have largely supplanted mechanical clocks for accuracy and precision in timekeeping. Horology itself has an incredibly long history and there are many museums and several specialised libraries devoted to the subject. Perhaps the most famous is the *Royal Greenwich Observatory*, also the source of the Prime Meridian (longitude 0° 0' 0"), and the home of the first marine timekeepers accurate enough to determine longitude.

The word 'clock' is derived from the Celtic words *clagan* and *clocca* meaning 'bell'. A silent instrument missing such a mechanism has traditionally been known as a timepiece, although today the words have become interchangeable. The clock is one of the oldest human interventions, meeting the need to consistently measure intervals of time shorter than the natural units: the day, the lunar month and the year. The current sexagesimal system of time measurement dates to approximately 2000 BC in Sumer. The Ancient Egyptians divided the day into two twelve-hour periods and used large obelisks to track the movement of the sun. They also developed water clocks, which had also been employed frequently by the Ancient Greeks, who called them 'clepsydrae'. The Shang Dynasty is also believed to have used the outflow water clock around the same time.

The first mechanical clocks, employing the verge escapement mechanism (the mechanism that controls the rate of a clock by advancing the gear train at regular intervals or 'ticks') with a foliot or balance wheel timekeeper (a weighted wheel that rotates back and forth, being returned toward its centre position by a spiral), were invented in Europe at around the start of the fourteenth century. They became the standard timekeeping device until the pendulum clock was invented in 1656. This remained the most accurate timekeeper until the 1930s, when quartz oscillators (where the mechanical **resonance** of a vibrating crystal is used to create an electrical signal with a very precise **frequency**) were invented, followed by atomic clocks after World War Two. Although initially limited to laboratories, the development of microelectronics in the 1960s made **quartz clocks** both compact and cheap to produce, and by the 1980s they became the world's dominant timekeeping technology in both clocks and wristwatches.

The concept of the wristwatch goes back to the production of the very earliest watches in the sixteenth century. Elizabeth I of England received a wristwatch from Robert Dudley in 1571, described as an arm watch. From the beginning, they were almost exclusively worn by women, while men used pocket-watches up until the early twentieth century. This was not just a matter of fashion or prejudice; watches of the time were notoriously prone to fouling from exposure to the elements, and could only reliably be kept safe from harm if carried securely in the pocket. Wristwatches were first worn by military men towards the end of the nineteenth century, when the importance of synchronizing manoeuvres during war without potentially revealing the plan to the enemy through signalling was increasingly recognized. It was clear that using pocket watches while in the heat of battle or while mounted on a horse was impractical, so officers began to strap the watches to their wrist.

The company H. Williamson Ltd., based in Coventry, England, was one of the first to capitalize on this opportunity. During the company's 1916 AGM it was noted that '...the public is buying the practical things of life. Nobody can truthfully contend that the watch is a luxury. It is said that one soldier in every four wears a wristlet watch, and the other three mean to get one as soon as they can.' By the end of the War, almost all enlisted men wore a wristwatch, and after they were demobilized, the fashion soon caught on - the British *Horological Journal* wrote in 1917 that '...the wristlet watch was little used by the sterner sex before the war, but now is seen on the wrist of nearly every man in uniform and of many men in civilian attire.' Within a decade, sales of wristwatches had outstripped those of pocket watches.

Now that clocks and watches had become 'common objects' there was a massively increased demand on clockmakers for maintenance and repair. Julien Le Roy, a clockmaker of Versailles, invented a face that could be opened to view the inside clockwork – a development which many subsequent artisans copied. He also invented special repeating mechanisms to improve the precision of clocks and supervised over 3,500 watches. The more complicated the device however, the more often it needed repairing. Today, since almost all clocks are now factory-made, most modern clockmakers *only* repair clocks. They are frequently employed by jewellers, antique shops or places devoted strictly to repairing clocks and watches.

The clockmakers of the present must be able to read blueprints and instructions for numerous types of clocks and time pieces that vary from antique clocks to modern time pieces in order to fix and make clocks or watches. The trade requires fine motor coordination as clockmakers must frequently work on devices with small gears and fine machinery, as well as an appreciation for the original art form. As is evident from this very short history of clocks and watches, over the centuries the items themselves have changed – almost out of recognition, but the importance of time-keeping has not. It is an area which provides a constant source of fascination and scientific discovery, still very much evolving today. We hope the reader enjoys this book.

PREFACE

WATCH design and construction has changed considerably during the past 50 years. The old verge, fusee, duplex, rack and pinion, full plate, and similar early styles of watches have gone. The cylinder watch formerly considered to be the ultimate has given way to the modern anchor or detached escapement with double roller. Watches are now much smaller, particularly in ladies' models, as well as thinner.

Many of the books which deal with watch repair are out-of-date in that they deal with the repair of watches which now exist only as heirlooms. The change in watch construction has invited the publication of an up-to-date book dealing with modern methods of repair, adjustment, and timing; and in this present book I have endeavoured to supply the need, and to include information on the adjustment of a watch for passing the Kew test. Whilst this volume chiefly deals with modern watches for which interchangeable parts are available, the practical information given applies equally to all types of watch, with the exception of the additional complicated mechanisms such as calendar, split seconds and repeater details. These additions to the train would require a special volume to themselves. The book is intended as a manual for all those interested in horology, professionally or otherwise. The book represents many years of practical experience with all types of watches. Regular articles on this subject appear in my monthly journal *Practical Mechanics*. The Advice Bureau run in connection with this paper undertakes to reply to readers' questions on this fascinating subject.

I wish to express my thanks to the Waltham Watch Company for permission to use certain illustrations and material relating to their watches; to the National Physical Laboratory for supplying details of their tests; to Mr. V. W. Clarke and the Editor of *The Watchmaker & Jeweller* for facts and illustrations relating to Hall-marks; to the Science Museum for permission to use illustrations of early watches; and to the proprietors of *Practical Mechanics* for permission to use illustrations and articles which appeared in the columns of that journal.

F. J. CAMM

CONTENTS

CHAPTER I

TIME AND THE ORIGIN OF WATCHES

DEVICES for measuring time go back to the earliest days. The Chinese invented probably the first form of clock—the Clepsydra or waterclock which consisted of a container filled with water having a float on the top. The water was allowed to drip from a small orifice so that as its level dropped the float followed it. A cord was attached to the float so that as it fell it pulled round an arbor to the end of which was attached a hand. Sundials, graduated candles, and similar devices have been used to mark the passage of time. The earliest astronomers observed that the earth took a year to make a revolution round the sun and 1 day to make 1 revolution round its own axis.

It was Julius Cæsar who made the effort to make the calendar year tally with the sun year, and he decided on a year of 12 months, the odd months having 31 days, and the even 30 excepting February which was to have only 29 with 30 every fourth year. It is common knowledge that a year consists of 365¼ days, so that every fourth year the four quarters would make an additional day which was added to the month of February. July took its names from Cæsar's christian name—the month of Julius. Augustus, the Roman Emperor, born in the eighth month, thought that one of the month's should be named after him. He borrowed February's 29th day and added it to August, thus bringing February to 28 days. Fifteen hundred years later it was discovered that the Julian system resulted in a loss of 11 minutes 10 seconds every year for the fifteen hundred years since the system was introduced. Thus, by the year 1532 there was a deficit of 11 days. To remedy this loss 11 days were dropped from the year 1532 and a new calendar was established which was lengthened by 5 hours 49 minutes. It was Pope Gregory XIII who introduced this, the Gregorian calendar, but he decided that rather than add the awkward figure of 5 hours 49 minutes to the year, he would add an extra day every 300 years.

England followed this example. On September 2nd, 1752, there was a gap of 11 days, so that when people went to bed on September 2nd they awoke on September 14th. It was in that year that January 1st was established as New Year's

Day. It is a popular belief that the Leap Year is every year that is divisible by four but the year 1900 was not a Leap Year. The year 2,000 will be. It is obvious that by adding a day every fourth year in the course of a century we have added almost a day too much, and therefore, the years which are divisible by 100 are not Leap Years unless they are also divisible by 400. Our day consists of 24 hours, but the Sidereal day is the time that elapses between two successive upper culminations of a fixed star of the vernal equinox. It is $\frac{1}{365}$th shorter than a solar day because the sun has changed positions slightly in that time and will not culminate quite so soon. Thus, there is the Sidereal hour, the Sidereal minute, and the Sidereal second, which have the same relations to the Sidereal day that the ordinary units do to the solar or 24-hour day. Each is 1/366th part shorter than the corresponding units of mean solar time.

We are not concerned, however, with these philosophical matters in this book which deals with watches, their adjustment and repair. Watches were first produced centuries ago, and have successively passed through various systems before finally reaching the present lever or anchor escapement. The ancient day and night were each divided into twelve equal divisions or hours, and as the relative lengths of the day and night varied according to the season of the year, so the length of each hour varied according to the season. For nearly 3,000 years the waterclock, the sun-shadow clock, or sun-dial, the sand-glass, and the burning candle, were the only devices known for time measurements, and it was not until the fourteenth century that the earliest known mechanical clock was constructed. The name of the first inventor is unknown, but it is certain that the clock which until 1872 was in the Tower of Dover Castle is one of the earliest practical clocks, and it is certainly the earliest still in working order. It was probably made in about 1395, and it was certainly in existence in 1405. It may be seen working at the Science Museum, South Kensington.

I mention this clock because its construction is of considerable interest and led the way to the early watch escapement. All of the early clocks and watches until 1750 were fitted with the same style of escapement as is fitted to the Dover Castle Clock. It is known as the verge. In this example the balance arm or foliot was not fitted with a spring, but carried two heavy lead blocks which swung through an angle of about 90 degrees under the action of the escape wheel. From Fig. 64, page 43, it will be seen that the pointed teeth of the escape wheel engage two pallets on the shaft of the foliot. The pallets are placed at right angles to each other, and the whole action of swinging the foliot, stopping and reversing the swing, is transmitted through the pallets. Variations in the individual teeth spacing, in friction and in the driving force causes the time of vibration to vary considerably with the verge and accurate timekeeping is almost impossible. It was in 1670 that Huygens adapted the pendulum to the control of the clock. The properties of the pendulum had been discovered nearly half a century earlier by Galileo while comparing the swinging of a lamp pendant with the beating of his pulse during a service in Pisa Cathedral. Huygens found that the isochronism (or equal time periods) of Galileo's pendulum is approximate only, and is only exact when the arc remains constant. As the verge escapement was still the only one known, and as this demanded an arc of vibration of at least 60 degrees, the timekeeping still left a great deal to be desired.

Fig. 1.—View of one of John Harrison's chronometers made in 1759.

The invention of the anchor escapement by Dr. Robert Hooke in 1675 made it possible to use a pendulum which swung through a small arc only and thus enabled far greater accuracy to be obtained. This was the same Hooke who discovered the law relating the action of forces with the deflection of springs, and he also discovered the coupling for shafts which are not in line, known as Hooke's joint or the universal joint. The early clocks were invariably driven by means of a weight, and it was only the invention of the mainspring by Peter Henlein of Nuremburg at the end of the fifteenth century that made possible the construction of a watch. The first watch escapements were of the verge type, and the amount of space occupied by this escapement caused the watch to be approximately spherical in shape, a fact which resulted in them being termed Nuremburg eggs.

The uncontrolled verge escapement, however, was entirely unsuited to the varying driving torque exerted by the mainspring, and it is to be feared that the first watches were toys rather than timekeepers. When the spring was fully wound, the powerful torque would cause the balance arm to swing

Fig. 2.—Two 18th-century pocket chronometers.

through a much larger angle than when the spring was almost unwound, and consequently the watch would lose time.

In order to obtain a constant driving torque, and so improve the timekeeping, a device known as the "fusee" was invented about 1525. This device may still be seen in many clocks to-day, and it is invariably used in marine chronometers. The principle may be clearly understood from Fig. 15. The mainspring is contained in a cylindrical drum, or barrel, on which is wound a length of slender chain composed of flat links. The other end of the chain is wound on a spiral drum, so contrived that as the spring runs down and becomes weaker, the leverage on the axis of the spiral increases, thus giving a practically constant torque throughout the range of the spring.

Even the invention of the fusee did not make the verge watch into a reliable timekeeper, and little improvement was made for nearly 150 years until the balance spring or "hair-spring" was invented by Hooke in 1660. The balance spring did for the watch what the pendulum had done for the clock, for the addition of the hairspring gave the balance wheel a definite period of oscillation, and although the shortcomings of the verge escape-ment interfered and prevented perfect iso-chronism, yet a vast improvement was achieved, and it now only required an im-proved escapement to make the watch a reliable instrument. The less the escape-ment interferes with the free swinging of the balance, the closer is the approximation to isochronism, and the best escapements are those which release the escape wheel, and give the impulse to the balance or pendulum, as nearly as possible at the middle of the swing.

Fig. 3.—*John Harrison's famous chrono-meter—his fourth.*

The first big improvement in escapements was made by George Graham in 1725, with his cylinder escapement shown on page 62. This was followed in 1755 by the detached lever escapement invented by Mudge. The latter, except for a few cylinder watches, is the only escapement now used. Such was the conservatism of watchmakers, however, that the verge continued in use until the middle of the last century.

Although many improvements in detail construction have been made during the last 100 years, it must be frankly admitted that the watch of to-day is an invention of the eighteenth century. Few important changes have taken place since then, and, in fact, the only triumph of recent years has been the marvellous development of watchmaking machinery which renders possible the purchase of an excellent watch for a few shillings and a really accurate timepiece for £10.

The most notable improvements during the last century have included the introduction of the keyless mechanism, the pull-out (positive and negative), hand-set mechanism in place of the side-set, the micrometric regulator, chronograph and split-seconds mechanisms, complicated mechanisms such as repeaters, calendars, phases of the moon, date, and alarm mechanisms; a wide variety of compensating balances; the invention of the overcoil hairspring by Breguet; the introduction of jewel holes to prevent wear; the use of invar, elinvar, palladium and other materials not greatly affected by temperature for hairsprings, whilst watches have grown progressively thinner. It will be seen that improvements since the introduction of the anchor escapement have chiefly concerned details. The modern standard of accuracy of timekeeping is, of course, far in advance of anything known one hundred years ago. We owe this accuracy really to the pioneer work of John Harrison whose chronometers can still be seen at the South Kensington Museum. Over two hundred years ago navigation was entirely a matter of guesswork. All that the navigator could do was to keep as accurate a check as he could of the courses steered and the distances travelled, making allowances for leeway, bad steering, currents and tides. This often resulted in shipwreck. It is relatively easy to ascertain latitude from observations of the sun or stars, but the determination of longitude is quite another matter. Latitude is the angular distance of a point north or south of the Equator, while longitude is the angular distance east or west of the Meridian of Greenwich.

In 1713 a Committee was appointed by the Government to consider the whole question of finding longitude at sea, and in the course of their work the committee, which later became known as the Board of Longitude, consulted Sir Isaac Newton. Newton told them that one method "is by a Watch to keep time exactly: but by reason of the Motion of a Ship, the Variation of Heat and Cold, Wet and Dry, and the Difference in Gravity in different latitudes, such a Watch hath not yet been made."

In Newton's time, as he remarks, no timekeeper known was capable of going with anything like the requisite accuracy under sea conditions, and it is clear that he regarded the construction of a suitable mechanism not far removed from

Fig. 4.—Four Key-wind Verge Movements, made about 1700. Note the ornate decoration of the plates and balance cocks. Whilst they were excellent examples of craftsmanship they were poor timekeepers.

Fig. 5.—Two 18th-century English cylinder watches.

impossibility. He went on to describe various other possible methods, but admitted that one and all were impractical at sea, and the board of Longitude, in desperation, succeeded in persuading the Government to offer a substantial reward for any "generally practicable and useful method of finding longitude at sea." The reward was to be graduated from £10,000 to £20,000 according to the magnitude of the error, and to obtain the maximum sum of the inventor had to devise a method which would be accurate within thirty miles at the end of a voyage lasting six weeks. Other nations had previously made similar offers, but this reward of £20,000 was by far the largest, and it had the additional distinction of being the only reward of its kind which was ever paid.

The cleverest clockmakers and scientists had failed to find a solution after trying for nearly twenty years, when John Harrison, the son of a Yorkshire carpenter, arrived in London. Harrison had been brought up to follow his father's trade, but mechanisms attracted him at any early age, and without ever serving an apprenticeship to any clockmaker, he managed to acquire sufficient knowledge to repair and even to construct a number of clocks. Who would have thought that this son of a humble Yorkshire carpenter was destined to solve the problem and win the reward, thus becoming the first and most famous maker of marine chronometers who has ever lived?

Harrison's object in coming to London was to enlist the aid of the Board of Longitude in the construction of a timekeeper for which he had already prepared the plans. His limited resources prevented him undertaking the construction unaided, and in his ignorance he hoped for assistance from the Board of Longitude. He was disappointed, for the Board refused to grant him a single penny and so nearly thwarted the only reasonable design which had ever been offered to them. Fortunately, however, Harrison was received courteously by the Astronomer Royal, the celebrated Halley, who gave him an introduction to a famous London clockmaker, George Graham, "Honest Graham" as he was known, was also a Northcountryman who was as generous as he was honest; he advanced Harrison the necessary funds without security or interest, and one cannot but regret that Graham was resting in Westminster Abbey long before he could witness Harrison's eventual success.

With Graham's loan in his pocket, Harrison returned to Barrow and spent the next six years in constructing his first

Fig. 8.—A divided ¾ plate movement of Elgin (American) make. It has exposed keyless work, and the regulator is inverted to provide further protection for the balance. The case has a screwed back and bezel.

Fig. 6 (below).—A Waltham (American) divided ¾ plate pocket watch with micrometric regulator, and exposed keyless work.

Fig. 7.—A Ditisheim (Swiss) bar movement with submerged keyless work and micrometric regulator. This watch obtained a Kew "A" certificate with 78 marks, and forms, with other watches illustrated in this chapter, part of the author's collection. See illustration of certificate on pages 132 and 133.

chronometer. It is just over two hundred years since its construction was completed in 1735, and, thanks to the patience and skill of Lt.-Cdr. R. T. Gould, R.N. (Retd.), in restoring Harrison's machines in recent years, not only the first but all five are working to-day in the Science Museum at South Kensington.

In his effort to attain absolute constancy of rate, Harrison saw the necessity of taking the most extreme precautions against friction, temperature errors, and the disturbing effect of the motion of the ship. In consequence, he embodied numerous devices of great originality and his eventual success was entirely due to his skill in inventing and constructing ingenious mechanical devices. His first timekeeper is the most simple of the five, but most of the constructional features are typical and merit a brief description.

The balance system was a duplicate one consisting of massive brass arms and brass weights. The balance arms were mounted on anti-friction areas of large radius, and were connected together by means of thin cross wires which ran on brass arcs attached to the balance arms. This arrangement caused them to swing as though geared together but with negligible friction, and it had the merit that the period of the balance system was practically unaffected by the motion of the ship.

The balance system was controlled by four helical springs, the tension in which was varied by a triple linkage of brass and steel rods in order to provide the requisite temperature compensation, and it is of interest to note that this was the first occasion upon which a temperature compensating device had ever been used in a timekeeper. All the wheels of the train, with the exception of the escape wheels, were constructed of oak, and the teeth, which were also of oak, were mortised into the rims. The teeth of one wheel meshed with little anti-friction rollers of lignum vitae on the next wheel in the train, and every wheel was mounted on anti-friction rollers.

Of the many possible causes of serious inaccuracy in a timekeeper, one of the most important is due to the variation of the angle through which the balance swings as the mainspring torque reduces between the intervals of rewinding. In all Harrison's later chronometers and in every chronometer which has been made since, this is avoided by the incorporation of an arrangement known as a "remontoire". In this arrange-

Fig. 11.—The well-known International watch movement. This is of the bar type with submerged keyless work.

Fig. 9 (below).—The mechanism of a ¼ repeater movement chiming the hours and quarters. This is arranged behind the dial. Such watches are seldom made now, but are in demand among collectors. There are also minute repeaters, which chime the hours, quarters, and minutes. The repeating mechanism is actuated by pushing a slide at the side of the case.

Fig. 10.—The split-seconds mechanism of a high-grade chronograph—the Longines. It is fitted with an Elinvar hairspring and uncut monometallic balance. The two centre seconds hands are superimposed and rotate together, but one may be stopped while the other runs on.

ment the balance and escapement are maintained in operation by a separate spring which is rewound at very frequent intervals by the mainspring. Rewinding occurs every few minutes at fixed intervals, and thus the actual driving torque is maintained at a practically constant value. Harrison's first timekeeper, however, did not incorporate a remontoire, but depended on a fusee for maintaining an approximately even torque. A fusee is not nearly so perfect as a remontoire, but is far less complicated.

Having successfully completed the first timekeeper—one might also call it a "machine", for it weighs over 70 lb.— Harrison tested it on a barge in the Humber and then brought it to London in 1736. The Admiralty decided to test it on a voyage to Lisbon, and Harrison accordingly embarked with it on H.M.S. *Centurion*. The correspondence between the First Lord of the Admiralty and the Captain of H.M.S. *Centurion* is worth quoting:

"ADMIRALTY,
"*14th May*, 1736

"To CAPTAIN GEORGE PROCTOR,
    "The Instrument which is put on Board your Ship has been approved by all the Mathematicians in Town that have seen it (and few have not), to be the Best that has been made for measuring Time: how it will succeed at sea you will partly be a Judge . . . The Man is said by those who know him best to be a very ingenious and sober Man, and capable of finding out something more than he has already, if he can find encouragement. I desire, therefore, that you will see the Man be used civilly, and that you will be as kind to him as you can."

"H.M.S. *Centurion*, at Spithead,
"*17th May*, 1736.

"To ADMIRALTY,
    "I am very much honoured by yours of the 14th, in Relation to the Instrument I carried out, and its maker: the Instrument is placed in my cabin, for giving the Man all the Advantage that is possible for making his Observations, and I find him to be a very sober, a very industrious, and withal a very modest Man, so that my good Wishes can but attend him: but the Difficulty of Measuring Time truly, where so many unequal shocks and motions stand

in opposition to it, gives me concern for the honest Man, and makes me feel he has attempted Impossibilities: but, Sir, I will do him all the Good, and give him all the help, that is in my Power, and acquaint him with your Concern for his success, and your Care that he shall be well treated. . . ."

The chronometer must have behaved excellently, for the Certificate which was given to Harrison after the voyage reads:

"When we made land, the said land, according to my reckoning (and others) ought to have been the Start; but, before we knew what land it was, John Harrison declared to me and the rest of the ship's company that, according to his observation with his machine, it ought to be the Lizard—the which, indeed, it was found to be, his observations showing the ship to be more West than my reckoning, above one degree and twenty-six miles."

Considering that this was the first trial ever made at sea, the success was a remarkable performance. While dead reckoning resulted in an error of about seventy miles after only a few days at sea on a well-known route, the error of Harrison's chronometer was practically negligible. In consequence of the excellent report on the chronometer, the Board of Longitude began to advance small sums to Harrison for the construction of improved versions. In 1737–39, Harrison constructed No. 2, an even heavier but more compact instrument with a number of important mechanical refinements. It is fitted with a remontoire mechanism, and Commander Gould has declared his belief that it was capable of winning at least the £10,000 award.

No. 2 was never tested at sea. Britain was at war with Spain at the time and there was a risk that it might fall into enemies' hands. I should perhaps mention that No. 1 never went to sea again after the voyage to Lisbon, but it demonstrated the excellence of Harrison's workmanship by going continuously for over thirty years in Harrison's house. It was never stopped once for cleaning or oiling during the whole period.

Between the years 1740 and 1757, Harrison constructed a third instrument. Both in construction and operation, it is fundamentally different in design to the two previous timekeepers, and mere words are inadequate to describe the perfection of workmanship and mechanical detail which Harrison incorporated. A close examination is necessary to appreciate the real beauty of the instrument, which, from the mechanical point of view, is almost perfect.

The bar type balance arms used in the previous instruments were replaced by a pair of large balance wheels connected, as before, by cross wires. A remontoire mechanism is fitted which rewinds every thirty seconds and is so devised to give an absolutely constant torque at the escape wheel. It is probably the most perfect remontoire mechanism ever made.

In 1757, Harrison informed the Board of Longitude that he would shortly be ready to compete for the £20,000 reward, but he suggested that before doing so, he should construct a much smaller timekeeper to serve as a check on the main one. His proposal was approved and Harrison, with the aid of his son, constructed his fourth chronometer—the most famous timekeeper which has ever been made.

It is very much smaller than the earlier instruments and is really a large watch, just over five inches in diameter. Even although No. 4 was only intended as an auxiliary to the main instrument, Harrison lavished almost unbelievable pains upon its design and construction. It is perhaps not altogether surprising, therefore, that it turned out to be just as perfect a timekeeper as was No. 3, and it had, of course, the very great advantage of being very much lighter and more portable. As a result, No. 3, which had taken Harrison seventeen years to perfect, was put aside and almost forgotten. It was never tested at sea.

No. 4 underwent its first sea test in 1761 on a voyage to Jamaica in H.M.S. *Deptford*. The course had been set to touch at Madeira, and after nine days at sea there was a discrepancy of 1½ degrees in the longitude as indicated by dead reckoning and by No. 4. This was a serious matter, for it might mean missing Madeira altogether.

However, Harrison insisted that the chronometer was correct, and said that provided the longitude of Madeira was correctly marked on the charts they would sight the island the next day. The Commander, Captain Digges, offered to bet Harrison five to one that the chronometer was wrong, but he held to Harrison's course and the island was sighted the following morning—much to the relief of the ship's company.

On reaching Jamaica after a nine weeks' voyage, the total error of the chronometer was only five seconds, corresponding

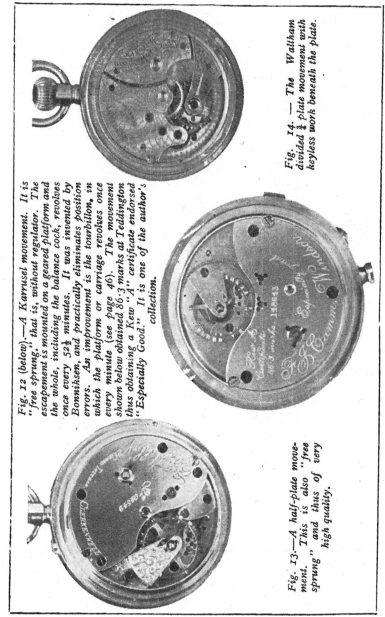

Fig. 14. — The Waltham divided ¾-plate movement with keyless work beneath the plate.

Fig. 12 (below).—A Karrusel movement. It is "free sprung," that is, without regulator. The escapement is mounted on a geared platform and the whole, including the balance cock, revolves once every 52½ minutes. It was invented by Bonniksen, and practically eliminates position errors. An improvement is the tourbillon, in which the platform or carriage revolves once every minute (see page 46). The movement shown below obtained 86·3 marks at Teddington thus obtaining a Kew "A" certificate endorsed "Especially Good." It is one of the author's collection.

Fig. 13.—A half-plate movement. This is also "free sprung," and thus of very high quality.

to less than one mile. Provided, therefore, that Harrison could show that his timekeeper constituted a "generally practicable and useful method of finding longitude at sea", he was entitled to the full award of £20,000. It was to prove almost easier to make the chronometers, however, than to wring the reward out of a reluctant and obstinate Board of Longitude. They paid him £2,500 but stubbornly refused to pay another penny until further trials had taken place. They claimed that the longitude of Jamaica was not precisely known, and seem to have believed that the astonishing accuracy of the timekeeper was due to a fortuitous cancellation of errors.

A second trial took place in 1764, on a voyage to Barbados. This time, the total error of the chronometer was 38 seconds fast, corresponding to 9½ miles, but, allowing for the slight temperature correction which Harrison had declared beforehand, the gross error at the end of a five months' voyage was only a loss of 15 seconds.

The Board of Longitude, however, would still not give way, although they finally agreed to pay a further £7,500 provided that Harrison gave a sworn declaration of the mechanism to a responsible committee. They refused to pay the final £10,000 unless Harrison made two more chronometers of equal performance.

Harrison was now over seventy years of age, and his sight was failing. He was eventually paid the £7,500, but he regarded the final instalment of £10,000 as lost for ever. He did, in fact, manage to construct one more instrument which is almost an exact copy of No. 4, but with less ornamentation. The Board of Longitude had evidently got a little common sense left, for they then commissioned Larcum Kendall, a well-known London watchmaker, to make a copy of No. 4, which he did at a cost of £450. The very remarkable performance of Kendall's copy was a most striking vindication of Harrison, and it was used by Captain Cook in his second and third Antarctic voyages between 1772 and 1777.

Still the Board would not give way, and it was not until Harrison found a supporter in the person of King George III that the Board were placed on the defensive. The King used his influence in Parliament, to whom Harrison presented a petition. Difficult questions were asked and the Board's outrageous treatment of Harrison was exposed. A full debate of the House nearly took place, when the Board gave way before the storm of indignation and paid the remaining balance.

Harrison had won his battle; he had proved himself the first and foremost maker of marine chronometers of all time, and we cannot but feel sincere regret that the old man, who had devoted the whole of his life in the interests of the safety at sea, should have lived so short a while afterwards to enjoy the benefits of his reward. John Harrison died in 1776 at the age of eighty-two, only three years after receiving the final instalment. Harrison had solved the problem which had baffled Halley, Newton, Leibnitz, and hundreds of others, and, working in the face of complete scepticism, Harrison had devoted fifty years to its solution.

Such was John Harrison's service to Humanity; he was a man to whom we, as the greatest maritime nation, should be deeply grateful, and of whom, as his own countrymen, we must be immensely proud.

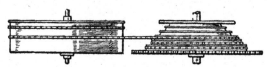

Fig. 15.—The fusee and mainspring barrel.

Interesting Facts.—Most modern watches make 5 ticks every second, and the following table shows the great amount of work the balance-wheel has to do:

> 300 ticks per minute;
> 18,000 ticks per hour;
> 432,000 ticks per day;
> 157,680,000 ticks per year.

The average size of a balance wheel is 0·62 in., so that in each vibration it will travel 2·343 in. In 1 hour it will travel 43,812 in., or 3,651 ft., and in a complete day will travel 87,624 ft., or 16·95 miles. If you had to walk that distance and failed to do so merely by 10 ft., it would be a matter of no moment, but if your watch fails by this amount it would be equivalent to a loss of $9\frac{1}{5}$ seconds a day, or nearly 5 minutes a month.

In some of the smallest watches a 22,000 or even a 36,000 train may be employed. The old English lever has a 15,000 train, and sometimes a 14,400 train (250 and 240 vibrations per minute respectively). A watch should be wound only once each day, at a regular hour, and preferably in the morning.

CHAPTER II

TOOLS AND MATERIALS

GOOD tools and an adequate supply of materials are essential for successful watch repairing. Most watches to-day are made on the interchangeable basis so that broken parts can be replaced without having to be turned or machined. It is not necessary usually to carry a stock of such replacement parts unless the watch repairer is an agent for a particular brand. It is, however, necessary to carry a good supply of various types of glasses of the crystal, empire, lunette, hunter, demi-hunter, button, and wrist-watch varieties, as well as a stock of hands of all types including spade, double-spade, cathedral, moon, and straight hour and minute hands, as well as a stock of seconds hands. Also obtain a good stock of first quality mainsprings in various strengths and in various lengths (they are sold according to the number of coils) to suit the general run of pocket and wrist-watches, a supply of hairsprings, small timing washers, assorted screws, transmission wheels for key-less work, winding shafts and buttons, pallet stones, jewel holes, balance staffs, ruby impulse pins, balance screws, hour and minute wheels, cylinders, sticks of blue steel in assorted sizes, sticks of brass in assorted sizes, hairspring collets, taper pins for fastening hairsprings, and a supply of the various sizes of pinion wire. These materials will cover the normal run of repairs. In practice it will be found that the general run of watch repairs comprises new balance staffs, new hands, new glasses, new hairsprings, and new winding staffs and buttons. Dial repairs are best put out. Cracked enamel dials, if the trouble is not extensive, can be repaired by means of a special white enamel which melts at a low temperature, but a badly cracked dial will have to be re-enamelled, and that is the work of a specialist. Metal dials which show a tendency to fade can be re-written and renovated very cheaply. Case repairs are dealt with in a separate chapter.

Tools should be selected carefully, and only the best should be bought, for they are the cheapest in the long run. Tweezers are available in a variety of styles and shapes. A cheap pair of hollow tweezers of the Boley pattern will suit for picking up small parts, but for hairspring work a special set of

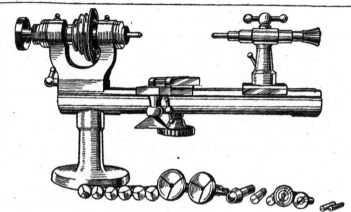

Figs. 16 & 17.—Watchmaker's lathe and some of the split collet and stepped chucks.

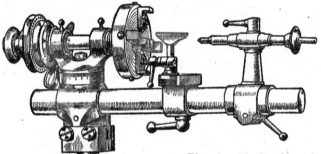

Fig. 18.—The Lorch watchmaker's lathe.

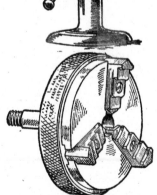

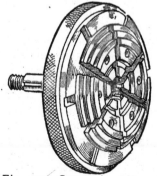

Fig. 19.—Concentric self-centring 3-jaw chuck with reversible jaws.

Fig. 20.—Concentric self centring 6-jaw chuck with reversible jaws, for holding bezels, thin discs, etc.

hand-forged tweezers should be bought and kept entirely for that work. Several pairs of good pliers, a pair of end cutters, a pair of side cutters, a pair of sliding tongs, and a pair of adjustable clamps for holding small work during soldering are essential tools to purchase first. A stock of watchmaker's screwdrivers in all sizes should be kept.

A set of broaches is necessary for opening out small holes in hands and other parts, as well as a collet-jaw broach-holder. A set of drills for use either in the bow-head or the lathe are necessary, as well as a set of watchmaker's files, a set of taps and dies, set of gravers, carborundum stone and oil stone, box of diamantine, red stuff (both the latter are used for polishing pivots), a burnisher for pivots, a split collet pin-holder, a jeweller's vice, a vice stake, watchmaker's hammer, and set of punches, balance poising callipers, a douzième gauge, a pivot gauge, fine centre punch, set of watchmaker's odd legs, internal and external callipers, pair of dividers, stainless steel rule graduated in 100ths, a watch-size gauge, a watch oiler, bottle of first quality watch oil, jewel setting outfit, blow-lamp for soldering and silver soldering, a supply of silver solder, lengths of brass wire in various gauges, metal saw, pair of jeweller's snips, pair of sliding jaw callipers, set of scrapers, a hand vice, tap wrench, set of punches and stake, supply of borax for silver soldering, brushes and chalk for cleaning, assorted trays, benzine for cleaning, a 1-in. micrometer, mainspring gauge, wire and sheet metal gauge, pegwood for cleaning, a hand drill, soldering iron, mainspring winder, lantern type hand-vice for holding seconds hands, set of hand closers, eye glasses of differing lens powers, a watch lathe with equipment and a good steel square. There will also be the usual run of small engineer tools.

Needless to say, the workshop must be well lighted and dust proof. The work bench must be equipped with a swivelling electric light. The small material should be stored in the nests of drawers sold for the purpose. The room must be well-heated to prevent steel parts from rusting. The lathe should be driven by a fractional horse-power motor, or by treadle. For preference it should be attached to a separate lathe bench, and its equipment must include a draw spindle tail stock with taper hole for split chucks and taper shanks, set of split collets, self-centring chuck, an independent jaw chuck, a slide rest, a watch button chuck, set of lathe tools, a face plate, set of carriers, set of stepped chucks, a drill chuck, pivoting plate,

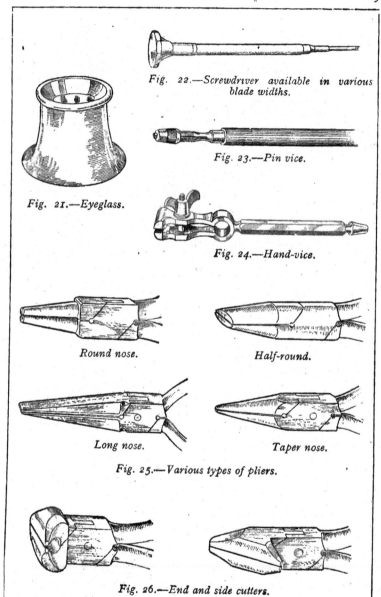

Fig. 22.—*Screwdriver available in various blade widths.*

Fig. 23.—*Pin vice.*

Fig. 21.—*Eyeglass.*

Fig. 24.—*Hand-vice.*

Round nose.

Half-round.

Long nose.

Taper nose.

Fig. 25.—*Various types of pliers.*

Fig. 26.—*End and side cutters.*

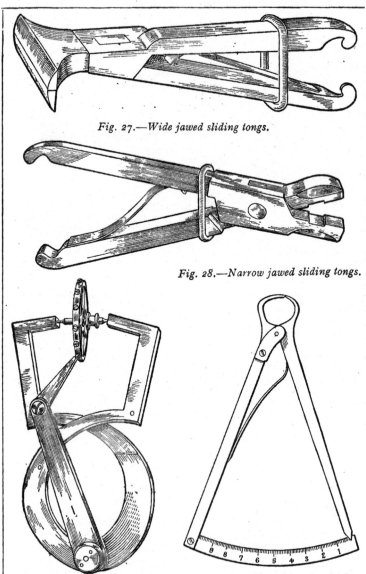

Fig. 27.—*Wide jawed sliding tongs.*

Fig. 28.—*Narrow jawed sliding tongs.*

Fig. 30.—*Balance poising callipers. The middle finger checks lateral truth of balance.*

Fig. 29.—*Douzième gauge for thickness, staff height, pinion height, etc.*

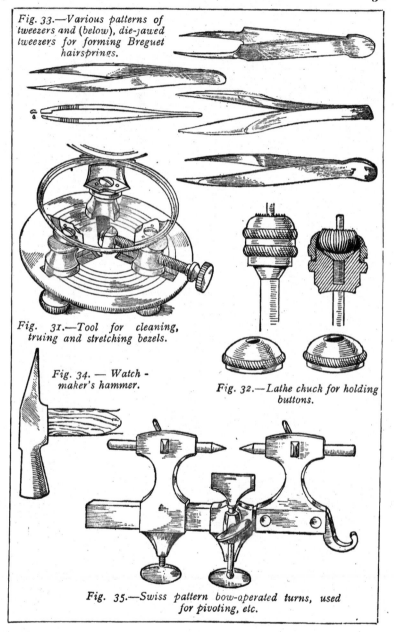

Fig. 33.—*Various patterns of tweezers and (below), die-jawed tweezers for forming Breguet hairsprings.*

Fig. 31.—*Tool for cleaning, truing and stretching bezels.*

Fig. 34. — *Watch - maker's hammer.*

Fig. 32.—*Lathe chuck for holding buttons.*

Fig. 35.—*Swiss pattern bow-operated turns, used for pivoting, etc.*

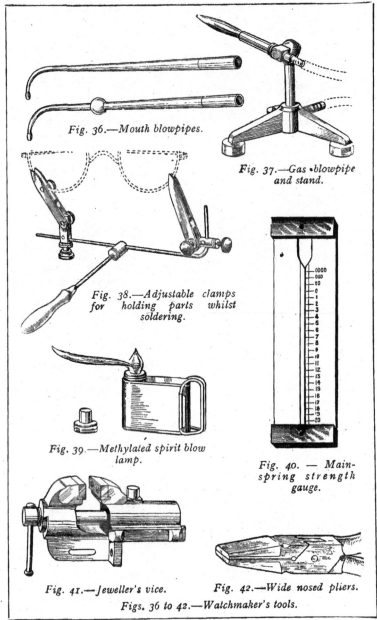

Fig. 36.—*Mouth blowpipes.*

Fig. 37.—*Gas blowpipe and stand.*

Fig. 38.—*Adjustable clamps for holding parts whilst soldering.*

Fig. 39.—*Methylated spirit blow lamp.*

Fig. 40. — *Main-spring strength gauge.*

Fig. 41.—*Jeweller's vice.*

Fig. 42.—*Wide nosed pliers.*

Figs. 36 to 42.—*Watchmaker's tools.*

hand rest, saw table, hand-turning tools, ring chuck, polishing head, saw spindle, and drill chuck for the head stock as well as a lever-operated tail stock spindle.

The watch tool and material dealers issue very complete catalogues showing the tools and materials available. Since Great Britain went off the gold standard tens of thousands of first grade watch movements have been removed from gold cases and can be purchased for a few shillings a dozen. A stock of these is useful, as a source of spares for watches which are not of the interchangeable variety or which have ceased to be made. Every watch repairer is expected to handle old watches for which materials are not now available including fusee, the verge, and the duplex styles. Old watch movements provide a fruitful source of materials.

A good workman does not blame his tools but it is impossible to do good work without good tools and it is a waste of good workmanship to exercise it on poor material. The great object should be to give extreme satisfaction to the customer, for reputations are easily made and lost in the watch repairing trade.

There are one or two excellent trade journals which will keep the repairer in touch with new lines and the news of the trade. Most of the tool and material dealers in London are either in Clerkenwell or Hatton Garden. There are, of course, some excellent dealers in the Provinces.

In ordering materials from the material dealers it is essential in order to obtain the correct part, to send the watch movement or the old part. Each watch manufacturer now makes so many dozens of different models using parts which look alike but differ in important details, that this is vital.

Where possible the make and size of the watch should be stated. There is a trade directory which gives the name of the agents and manufacturers for most of the standard makes of watches. It is published by the National Trade Press, Drury House, Russell Street, W.C.2, who also publish each month *The Watchmaker and Jeweller*. I recommend the reader to subscribe to this latter journal, and also to obtain their handbook and their list of trade marks. It is most helpful in placing the repairer in direct touch with the source of supply when material dealers may not be able to supply.

CHAPTER III

THE PARTS OF A WATCH

WITH high-class watches, one can expect a very close rate of time under both extreme and normal conditions, but the inexpensive watch, by reason of its condition, cannot be expected to keep time within several seconds a day. A keen student, however, will soon be able to classify the various grades and execute work accordingly. Any new parts

Fig. 43.—A modern Swiss lever movement of the popular 10½ ligne size (shown greatly enlarged).

should be faithfully copied, if it is not possible to obtain standard material, in order to maintain the standard of the watch. Good work always reflects credit on the repairer.

Special Names for Parts.—The first step is to become thoroughly acquainted with the numerous components of an ordinary watch. Many parts have special names, and to be conversant with them will often save considerable time when ordering new material. The enlarged illustration on the opposite page depicts a modern Swiss Lever movement of the popular 10½-ligne size.

"Lignes" and "sizes" are the measurements usually used to determine the size of a movement. In Fig. 44 are shown the various diameters of a movement. Of the two main dimensions that of the largest diameter is usually taken, and the most common measurement is the ligne. As 1 ligne equals approximately $\frac{3}{32}$ in. a 10½-ligne watch measures $\frac{15}{16}$ in. which is short of an inch. The American industry favours the "size" as a unit of measurement. Size O equals $1\frac{5}{30}$ in. Each size above size O increases by $\frac{1}{30}$ in., and a size below O decreases by $\frac{1}{30}$ in. 10½-ligne movements are to be found in both gentlemen's and ladies' wrist-watches. Until a few years ago this

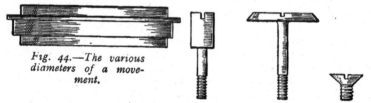

Fig. 44.—The various diameters of a movement.

Fig. 45.—Three different types of screw used in the construction of a watch.

size was almost universal in ladies' watches, and the cheaper watches still favour this size.

Number of Screws.—Some watches have as many as 150 separate pieces, and of this large number there are at least 35 screws. Fig. 45 shows three different types of screw: the cheese-headed plate screw, the flat-headed case screw, and the small jewel screw with countersunk head. The main frame of the movement consists of two plates: the bottom or dial plate and the top or back plate, which is visible when the case is opened. The modern back plate has changed from a circular plate into a number of sections usually called bars or bridges, thereby rendering the works easily accessible.

Almost half the movement is used for the large bar that supports the mainspring barrel, a thin cylindrical metal box with teeth around the outside edge. The barrel is fitted with a cover, and the axle upon which it rotates is called the arbor.

The arbor has a short hook which engages the inner eye of the mainspring.

The Great Wheel.—The barrel, or main driving wheel, is often referred to as the great wheel, and the other wheels are arranged in the following order. In the centre of the movement and driven by the barrel is the centre wheel; next, the 3rd wheel; then the 4th wheel (the seconds wheel); and finally the 5th wheel (the escape wheel). The remaining section is known as the escapement. When referring to the escapement, this is generally assumed to include the escape wheel, the small anchor-shaped piece called the lever, which arrests and releases the escape wheel tooth by tooth, and the balance and its kindred pieces.

The balance wheel is mounted on a slender axle—the balance staff. Fixed upon the staff above the balance wheel is the hair-spring and below the balance wheel is the roller. The roller is fitted with a small impulse pin, but when a jewelled pin is used it is commonly called the ruby pin. The function of the roller is to unlock the pallets. Fig. 46 shows the balance, balance staff and roller, and the position of the fork of the pallets with regard to the ruby pin.

Jewels.—In jewelled watches, the most popular number of jewels is 15. These jewels are not mere ornaments, but are used to minimise wear. The 15 jewels are always arranged in this order. Two each for the 3rd, 4th, and 5th wheels and pallets, 4 for the balance, 2 pallet stones and the ruby pin. Fig. 49 shows sections of plate and balance jewels. No. 1 is a section of the jewels used for 3rd, 4th, and escape wheels; No. 2 is an endstone; and No. 3 shows the arrangement of the balance jewels, one at each end of the balance staff. In high-class watches, jewel hole and endstone are fixed in separate settings and kept in position by 2 jewel screws as shown. It will be observed that the balance jewel hole differs slightly from the ordinary jewel hole. For example, the oil sink is inside on the balance hole and outside on the plate hole.

The pivots, the short projections of the pinions and staffs which actually rotate in the bearings also differ in shape. In Fig. 48 are depicted at *A* an ordinary pivot with a square shoulder and at *B* a balance pivot with a conical shoulder. Type *A* pivots are used with No. 1 type jewels. In high-class watches the lever and escape wheel pivots are often made conical and provided with balance type jewels and endstones.

The Bottom Plate.—Fig. 50 shows a bottom plate. This

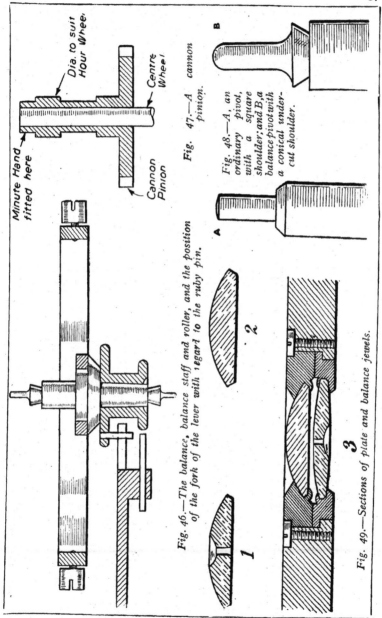

Dia. to suit Hour Wheel.

Centre Wheel

Minute Hand fitted here

Cannon Pinion

Fig. 47.—A cannon pinion.

Fig. 48.—A, an ordinary pivot, with a square shoulder; and B, a balance pivot with a conical under-cut shoulder.

B

A

Fig. 46.—The balance, balance staff and roller, and the position of the fork of the lever with regard to the ruby pin.

2

1

3

Fig. 49.—Sections of plate and balance jewels.

carries the small winding and hand-setting wheels and the levers that operate them. The winding shaft passes through two small wheels seen at the top, the top or crown wheel engages the smaller of the 2 flat steel wheels seen in Fig. 43 at right-angles. When winding, the mainspring is prevented from "running back" by the action of the pawl or click which arrests the larger of the winding wheels.

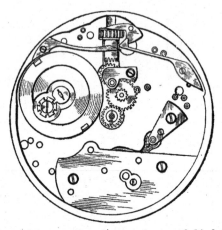

Fig. 50.—A bottom plate showing the parts behind the dial.
This movement is a Patek Phillippe.

The winding shaft is prevented from being pulled right out by the pull-up piece, which serves the dual purpose of retaining the winder and forcing down, by means of the return lever, the lower wheel on the winding shaft, causing it to engage the intermediate hand setting wheel. The intermediate wheel gears with the minute wheel—a flat brass wheel having a short pinion and rotating on a stud fixed in the plate—and the teeth of the minute wheel gear with those of the cannon pinion. The cannon pinion is really a small tube with teeth around the bottom and it fits friction tight on the extended pivot of the centre wheel. It is upon this tubular pinion that the minute hand is fixed.

When the winder is pulled out, it depresses the lever and the castle wheel, and the motion wheels (the hand wheels), are engaged and can be turned around to the desired position. Fig. 47 shows the cannon pinion.

CHAPTER IV

THE COMPENSATING BALANCE & HAIRSPRING

To illustrate the general principles of timing, it may be of interest first to make a comparison between the balance in a watch and the pendulum in a clock, as both of them evidently

Fig. 51.—Two bars of equal length when at normal temperature. The dotted lines indicate the relative expansions when each is heated to a similar degree.

Fig. 52.—The effect of heat on the bi-metallic bar. The greater expansion of the brass causes the bar to curve upward.

Fig. 53.—The two metals fused together.

Fig. 54.—If cold were applied instead of heat, the bar would curve in the opposite direction.

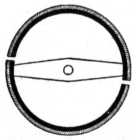

Fig. 55.—Watch balance in which the arms and inner portion of the rim are of steel. The outer portion is brass fused to the steel. The rim is severed at two points near the arm, permitting the rim to move under change of temperature.

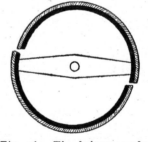

Fig. 56.—The balance under the influence of heat. It will be noticed that the free ends of the balance rim have curved inwards, thus reducing the diameter of the balance (radius of gyration).

perform the function of measuring or beating time. The pendulum, as we all know, requires no special spring to bring it to its centre line, the perpendicular, as the force of gravity furnishes the necessary power for doing this work in a very ideal way. When a pendulum is put in motion, it makes a vibration in a certain interval of time, and in proportion to its length, regardless of its weight, because the force of gravity acts on it in proportion to its mass. The length of a pendulum is reckoned from its centre of suspension to its centre of oscillation, which latter point is located a short distance below the middle of the bob. If a weight is added *above this point*, the clock will *gain*, because it raises the centre of oscillation and has the same effect on the time-keeping as raising the whole bob, which is equivalent to a shortening of the pendulum;

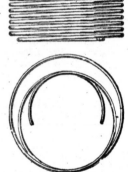

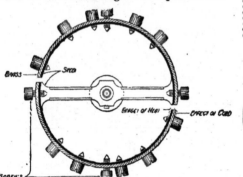

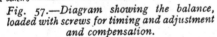

Fig. 57.—*Diagram showing the balance, loaded with screws for timing and adjustment and compensation.*

Fig. 58. — *Helical balance spring fitted usually to marine chronometers.*

but if a weight is added *below this point, it has the opposite effect,* as it really lengthens the pendulum. Reasoning from these facts we come to the conclusion that we can make a certain change in the rate of a clock in three different ways. For example, we may make it gain: (1) by raising the bob; (2) by adding weight above the centre of oscillation; and (3) by reducing the weight below that point. An interesting fact in relation to the pendulum, which may not be generally known among watchmakers, is that its rate of vibration varies slightly with change of latitude, and also of altitude (that is, its height above the sea-level), making a clock lose at the Equator and at high altitudes, and gain as we go nearer the sea-level and the Poles. This is due, partly to the distance from the centre of the earth, which is greater at the Equator than at the Poles, and partly to the centrifugal force resulting from the rotation of the earth on its axis. Both these factors tend to make an object weigh less (on a spring balance) at the Equator than at the Poles, and also cause a change in the rate of a clock as stated above. In view of these facts we might, as a fourth way of making a clock gain—although not a very practical one—move to a locality nearer the Pole. A balance is different from a pendulum in three fundamental points: first, it is poised; consequently the force of gravity has no effect on it, except as its influences the friction on its pivots; second, the vibrations are controlled by a spring instead of the force of gravity; third, a weight (mass) added to a balance will always make it vibrate slower, provided it is

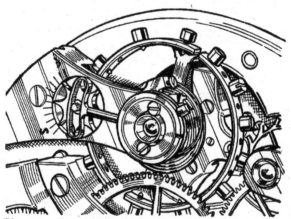

Fig. 59.—*The Waltham micrometric regulator. Other makers use an external rack and pinion, or a spring-loaded cam.*

not thereby put out of poise, and the retarding effect will be greater the farther the weight is placed away from its centre. One difficulty encountered in the first attempt to make accurate timepieces was the variation in the dimensions of metals caused by difference in temperature. All metals with the exception of a recently discovered alloy of steel and nickel (64 parts of steel and 36 of nickel) have the property of expanding with increase of temperature—the different metals showing a somewhat different rate of change. As the length of the pendulum is the all-important factor in the timing of clocks, so also is the diameter of the balance and the length and resiliency of the hairspring in a watch. It is absolutely necessary to

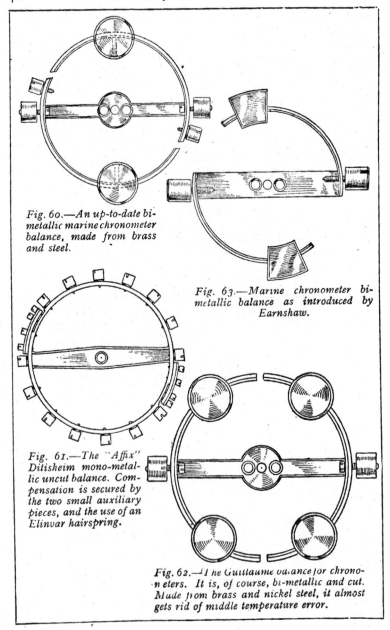

Fig. 60.—*An up-to-date bi-metallic marine chronometer balance, made from brass and steel.*

Fig. 63.—*Marine chronometer bi-metallic balance as introduced by Earnshaw.*

Fig. 61.—*The "Affix" Ditisheim mono-metallic uncut balance. Compensation is secured by the two small auxiliary pieces, and the use of an Elinvar hairspring.*

Fig. 62.—*The Guillaume balance for chrono-neters. It is, of course, bi-metallic and cut. Made from brass and nickel steel, it almost gets rid of middle temperature error.*

devise some means of compensating for changes in temperature before a reliable timepiece of either form can be made. So far as this problem applies to clocks, the mercury pendulum proves to be a very satisfactory solution, at least so far as

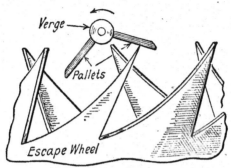

Fig. 64.—*The verge escapement—now obsolete.*

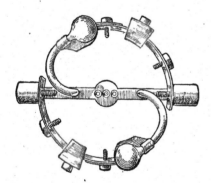

Fig. 65.—*The Loseby compensating balance; on each arm of the rim is a vessel containing mercury.*

Fig. 66.—*The Wyler compensating balance as fitted to the Wyler self-winding wristwatch. It is surrounded by a protecting rim, and is shockproof.*

accuracy is concerned. The bob of this pendulum is composed of one or more tubes of glass or iron, and these tubes are filled with mercury to a certain height. When of proper dimensions, the expansion and contraction of this column of mercury raises or lowers its mass to exactly compensate for the change in the length of the pendulum rod due to variations in the

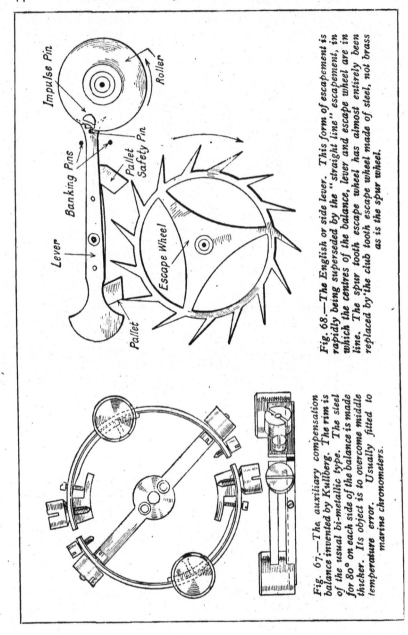

Fig. 68.—The English or side lever. This form of escapement is rapidly being superseded by the "straight line" escapement, in which the centres of the balance, lever and escape wheel are in line. The spur tooth escape wheel has almost entirely been replaced by the club tooth escape wheel made of steel, not brass as is the spur wheel.

Fig. 67.—The auxiliary compensation balance invented by Kullberg. The rim is of the usual bi-metallic type. The steel for 80° on each side of the balance is made thicker. Its object is to overcome middle temperature error. Usually fitted to marine chronometers.

temperature. This method, although very satisfactory for clocks, cannot, of course, be applied to watches, for obvious reasons, but for this purpose we make use of the property of the metals alluded to above, namely, *the difference* in the ratio of *expansion in different metals.*

A number of holes are drilled radially through the bimetallic rim, and these holes are tapped to receive the balance screws. Usually about twice as many holes are made in the

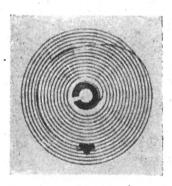

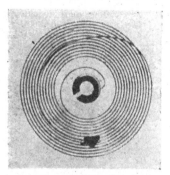

Fig. 69.—*The Overcoil hairspring, the outer curve of which is made to conform with Phillip's theory. It gives a concentric action to the hairspring and thus reduces position errors. Such an overcoil is often erroneously called "Breguet," which is a specially formed curve. It is impossible to eliminate position errors with a flat hairspring.*

Fig. 70.—*The Waltham hairspring showing inner and outer terminal curves. The inner curve shown in Fig. 69 tends to throw the spring out of poise during its vibrations. With the inner curve shown above, this tendency is eliminated. Waltham hairsprings are hardened and tempered in form. Most other springs are formed after the springs have been tempered.*

rim as the number of screws used in the balance; this is done to give opportunity for moving the screws in the final adjusting to temperatures. The object in using screws in the balance rim is two-fold; first, to provide the necessary weight (mass) in the rim, and second, to have this weight movable for temperature adjustments, as stated above.

We will now understand from what has been said that when a compensating balance is exposed to a higher temperature, every part of it expands, or grows larger, but as a result of the combination of the two metals in the rim, and the ends of the rim being free to move, each half of the rim will curve inward, carrying its weight towards the centre of the balance, and thus compensate for the lengthening of the arms and the weakening of the hairspring. If a balance is exposed to a lower temperature, the action will, of course, be in the opposite direction.

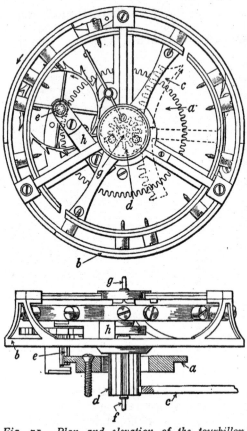

When a watch is to be adjusted to temperatures, it is run 24 hours, dial up, in a temperature of 90°F., and its rate compared with a standard. It is then run 24 hours, dial up, in a temperature of 40°F. If its shows a gain in the 40° temperature, as compared with the running in the 90°, it is said to be under - compensated. This is remedied by moving some screws nearer the free ends of the rim. This will, of course, result in a greater compensating effect, because the screws which we move nearer the ends of the rim must travel a greater distance in or out in relation to the centre of the balance when the balance is exposed to changes of temperature.

Fig. 71.—*Plan and elevation of the tourbillon escapement. The balance is mounted on a carriage which itself revolves once every minute, thus eliminating position errors. In this diagram* a *is the fourth wheel,* b *the revolving cage or carriage,* d *carriage pinion,* e *the escape pinion,* f *pivot for seconds hand,* h *escape cock,* g *upper pivot,* c *the third wheel gearing with* d. *The Karrusel, invented by Bonniksen, is somewhat similar except that it rotates once in* 52½ *minutes.*

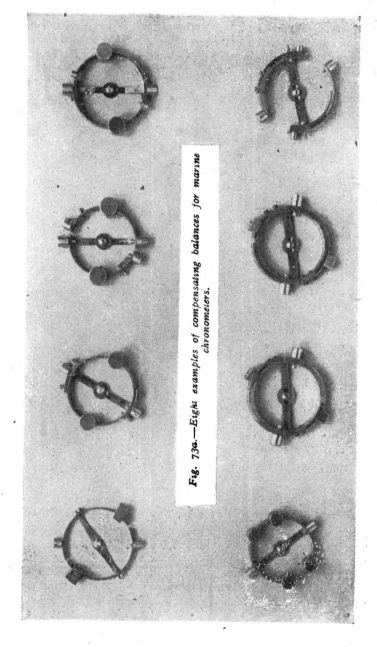

Fig. 73a.—Eight examples of compensating balances for marine chronometers.

After the screws have been moved, the movement is tried again the same length of time, and so on, until it runs the same in both temperatures. When a screw is moved in one side of the balance, it is, of course, necessary that the corresponding screw in the other side should be moved the same. A modern

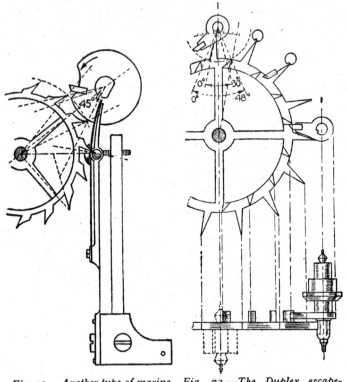

Fig. 72.—*Another type of marine chronometer escapement, as designed by Earnshaw. The disadvantage is that it tends to "set" or stop when worn in the pocket.*

Fig. 73.—*The Duplex escapement. This type was extremely popular at one time, and was finally fitted to the cheap Waterbury watches. It is now obsolete.*

compensation balance, combined with a correctly proportioned steel Breguet hairspring, which has been hardened and tempered in form, constitute a time-measuring device of marvellous accuracy. And the bi-metallic rim, hardened as the Waltham balances are, so as to be perfectly safe against distortion from ordinary handling, is certainly a boon to the watchmaker.

The mean time screws used in the Waltham balances furnish an excellent means for accurate timing, as two, on opposite sides, can be turned an equal amount in (making the watch run faster) or out (slower) without changing the poise of the balance.

The following is the approximate effect of *one-half turn* of two mean time screws:

18-size and 16-size	.. ..	$2\frac{1}{2}$ seconds per hour
Colonial series and 12-size	..	$2\frac{1}{2}$,, ,,
0 size and 3–0-size	.. ..	3 ,, ,,
Jewel series	..	$3\frac{1}{2}$,, ,,
10 Ligne	..	$3\frac{1}{2}$,, ,,

An illustration of a hairspring supplied with a theoretically correct outer terminal, commonly known to watchmakers by the name of Overcoil, is shown in Fig. 69.

As is well known to watchmakers, hairsprings are supplied with overcoils to secure a concentric action of the hairspring while the balance is in motion. A concentric action of the hairspring is necessary, in order to reduce the position error.

This result is partially obtained when a hairspring is supplied with a theoretically correct outer terminal or overcoil, whereby the centre of gravity of the outer half of the hairspring is made to coincide with the centre of the balance at every stage of its vibration.

In a watch fitted with a hairspring with an outer terminal curve only, there still remains a position error, part of which, at least, is due to the fastening of the inner end of the spring, which, in its ordinary form, tends to throw the spring out of poise during its vibrations.

This the Waltham Watch Company has succeeded in overcoming by making hairsprings with theoretically correct inner terminal curves. This inner curve maintains the body of the spring in perfect poise with the balance, during both its opening and closing vibrations. I show an illustration (Fig. 70) of a hairspring of this kind with inner and outer terminals.

The design of the hairspring having been perfected, there came the problem of properly producing these springs.

Flat hairsprings, that is to say, those without an overcoil, are only fitted to cheaper watches, although high-grade thin dress watches are sometimes fitted with them in order to reduce the thickness of the movements. It is impossible to eliminate position errors when a flat hairspring is fitted.

CHAPTER V

THE LEVER ESCAPEMENT

THE proper action of the human heart is no more essential to ensure a sound and healthy body, than is the proper adjustment and action of the escapement to the reliable performance of the watch. If the watch escapement is properly made and adjusted it will not only run—but will run with marvellous accuracy. So the timekeeping qualities of the watch are in large measure dependent on the condition of the escapement. It is therefore of great importance that every watchmaker should acquire an intimate knowledge of all the actions that are involved in the kinds of escapements with which he has anything to do.

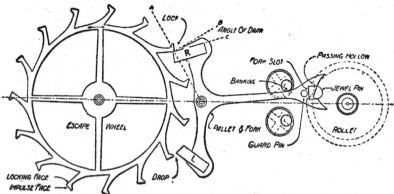

Fig. 74.—*All good watches have a lever escapement of the type shown here. Note the jewelled pallets.*

The only kind of escapement used in modern watches is the detached lever escapement, sometimes designated as the anchor escapement. This escapement requires no special introduction to watchmakers, for by extensive use, and by the test of time, it has been proved to be the most practical, as well as the most reliable form of escapement for pocket timepieces.

I include in this chapter some drawings of the lever escapement that they may be convenient for reference, and an aid to the clear understanding of the text.

The function of the escapement is to impart to the balance, regularly, and with as small loss as possible, the power which has been transmitted through the train from the mainspring to the escape pinion. In the lever escapement this is accomplished by means of two distinct actions: first, the action of the escape wheel and pallet; second, the action of the fork and roller pin. Fig. 74, given on page 50, is a plan view of the Waltham Lever Escapement, as used in the 16-size, and the 18-size models; movements drawn to scale 5-to-1, and

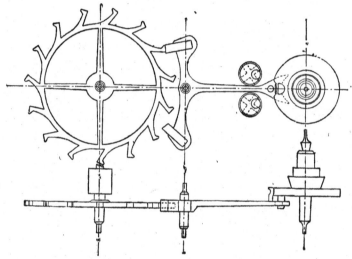

Fig. 75.—Lever escapement of the single roller type.

giving the names of the principal parts and features of the same. The escape wheel is mounted friction tight on the slightly tapered staff of the escape pinion. It has 15 teeth, called "Club Teeth" on account of their peculiar shape, resulting from the addition of impulse faces to the ends of the teeth, and to distinguish them from "ratchet teeth", the name given to a style of pointed teeth used on escape wheels in an earlier form of lever escapement. In descriptions of this escapement the term "exposed pallets" is used. This means that the pallet stones are visible, with the active ends standing out free from the body of the pallet, as distinguished from an earlier form of pallet with "covered stones" set in slots running in the plane of the pallet.

The Pallet Action.—The action of the escape wheel and pallet includes the following features: impulse, drop, lock, draft and slide, and in giving a general description of these actions we will consider briefly what constitutes each one of these features. The pallet is of the kind called "circular pallet", which means that the distance from the pallet arbor to the middle of the impulse face is the same for both pallet stones. Another kind of pallet is made with "equidistant lock", that is, the distance from the pallet arbor to the point

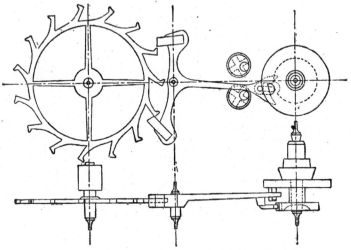

Fig. 76.—Lever escapement of the double roller type.

where the lock takes place, is the same for both pallet stones. The pallet is mounted on its arbor, which is located close to the periphery of the escape wheel. A theoretically correct distance in relation to the diameter of the escape wheel will not allow an excess of clearance between the pallet and the escape wheel teeth when opposite the pallet arbor, and for that reason the amount of stock in the pallet is made very small at that point. The pallet is slotted for the 2 pallet stones in such a way as to make the inside corners of the pallet stones reach over 3 teeth of the escape wheel, and to make the outside corners of the stones reach over 2 teeth and 3 spaces of the wheel, with a small amount of clearance in each instance, which is called the "drop".

One other important point in relation to the slotting is to direct the slots in the pallet in such a way as to make the locking faces of each pallet stone present to the locking corners of the escape wheel teeth a certain angle of "draw" when the stones are in the position of "lock". I will try to make this condition clear by referring to the drawing on page 50. Suppose that the escape wheel is being forced in the direction indicated by the arrow, but is prevented from turning in that direction because the locking face of the R pallet stone is directly in the way of a tooth. The particular tooth which is

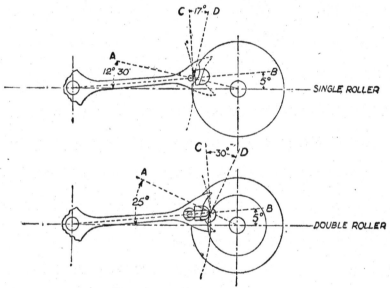

Figs. 77 & 78.—The safety action.

resting on the pallet stone is exerting a certain pressure directly towards the pallet arbor. If the locking face of the pallet stone were along the line B, which is at a right-angle to that line of pressure, there would be no tendency for the pallet to turn in either direction, but being along the line C, which forms an inclined plane in relation to the direction of the pressure, the pressure applied by the escape wheel tooth will tend to pull the pallet stone towards the escape wheel. This action is called the "draft" or "draw". The turning of the pallet is, however, limited by the banking pin, and the object of the draw is to keep the fork against the banking pin all the time that it is not in engagement with the jewel pin. This action of "draw" is similar on the L stone; the only differences are, first, that the pressure of the escape wheel tooth is exerted in the direction *away* from the pallet arbor, instead of towards it, and second, that the turning of the pallet, which in this instance is in the opposite direction, is limited by the other banking pin.

A glance at the drawing on page 50 will make it apparent that the impulse face, which is formed by the surface between the locking and the let-off corners, is at a different angle on the R from that on the L stone. The impulse angles of the stones in the escapement represented by this drawing are, on the R stone, 6° 30′, and on the L stone 14°. The above refers in each instance to the angle of the impulse face in relation to a right-angle to the locking face, or to the body of the stone. From this condition and from the direction of the pallet stones in relation to the body of the pallet, the factory names "straight" and "crooked" have been given to the R and L stones, respectively. In books and treatises on the lever escapement the names "receiving" and "discharging" are used, but when, as a matter of fact, both pallet stones perform the functions of receiving and discharging, one as much as the other, these names do not seem to be appropriate. For my part I prefer to use the letters R and L to distinguish one stone from the other, and these letters may easily be remembered as right and left, this being the order in which the stones appear as we look at the top of the pallet with the fork turned towards us.

The impulse or lift is divided between the escape wheel clubs and the pallet stones; the two together cause the pallet to turn through an angle of 8°30′.

The lock amounts to from 1° to 1° 30′, making the total angular motion of the pallet about 10°. This is the condition when the pallet is "banked to drop", that is, when the teeth of the escape wheel will just barely pass by the let-off corners of the pallet stones as the fork comes to rest against the bankings. A certain amount of clearance, or freedom, has to be added to this to allow for oil, etc., so that the bankings have to be turned away from the centre line a small amount to allow for what is called "slide", that is, the pallet stone will slide a visible amount into the escape wheel, after the escape wheel tooth drops on to the same. The amount of slide should, however, be very small, because it causes loss of power, by increasing the resistance to unlocking as, in order to un'ock, the escape wheel actually has to be turned backwards against the power of the mainspring, and the amount of this recoil is in proportion to the lock and slide added together. It is therefore important to notice the action of every tooth of the escape wheel on both pallet stones, to ascertain that each pallet stone has some slide on every tooth, and to allow only a small amount in the place where it appears to be closest.

Roller and Jewel Pin.—One problem in connection with lever escapements, with which every watchmaker has had more or less experience, has come to a final solution in the modern double roller escapement. This is the fastening of the jewel pin. The roller, which holds the jewel pin, is made of bronze, with a hole in it the shape of the pin, but a certain amount smaller than the pin. The jewel pin is made of sapphire, and is made slightly tapering, and is forced into the hole in the roller, thus making it permanently secure. The shape of the jewel pin is round, with one side flattened off to measure three-fifths of the diameter of the pin, and the sharp corners removed. This form of jewel pin is superior in general practice to any other form, as it unites strength with the most desirable shape at the points of action. The principle of setting the jewel pin directly in the roller, without cement, is made possible by the double roller escapement, because of the special roller for the safety action. It would not be practical to set jewel pins without cement in steel rollers, as it is in bronze, neither would it be advisable to use bronze rollers for the safety action, because it has been found by experience that tempered steel is better for that purpose. But by separating the two features, it makes a most desirable combination to use a bronze roller for carrying the jewel pin, and a separate steel roller for the safety action.

Matching the Escapement.—The term "matching the escapement" is used to designate the work of bringing the different parts of the escapement into correct relation to each other; in other words, to make the necessary moves in order to obtain the proper lock, draft, drop, slide, fork length, let-off, etc. The best way of learning to do this work is to have a competent instructor who is at hand ready to inspect and to give advice. The difficulties are not so great in *doing* this work. as in correctly determining *what* to do, in order to bring about certain results, and also to know when the escapement is in a proper condition. It is difficult to give in writing a comprehensive idea of how to do this work. I will, however, give a few points which I hope will be useful to the beginner.

The first thing to receive attention is the condition of the pivots on the escape pinion, pallet arbor and balance staff, to see that they are straight, and that they fit properly in their respective holes. It is abolutely necessary that each pivot should have *some* side-shake, but it is also very important to *guard against too much side-shake*, as such an excess causes loss of power and uncertainty in the action of the escapement. A desirable amount of end shake should be from ·02 to ·05 mm. As soon as these points have been found to be correct we are ready to try the "lock" and the "drop". In describing the pallet action, we made the clear statement that che lock should amount to from 1° to 1° 30'. This statement is, of course, of no practical use unless we are equipped with the necessary instruments for measuring this angle. We may, however, use the thickness of the pallet stones for comparison and obtain practically the same results, by making the amount of lock equal to $\frac{1}{10}$ to $\frac{1}{8}$ the thickness of the stone, from the locking to the let-off corner. This corresponds very closely to the above angular measurements. If the pallet stones are to be moved, in order to change the amount of lock, it is very important to first consider what will be the effect of a certain move, besides the alteration of the lock. The drop, for example, is effected very rapidly by moving the L stone. Hence if the drops are equal, we should make the change in the lock by moving the R stone. If the lock is too strong, and the drop is largest on the outside, the L stone should be moved. If the lock is too strong, and the drop is the largest on the inside, it is necessary to move both stones. Move the L stone out a small amount, and move the R stone in until the lock is correct. It is also well to recognise that the drop may be modified to a certain extent by moving the pallet stones, close to one or the other side, in the slots; as there is always some room allowed for the shellac which is used for holding the stones. The moving of the pallet stones in or out in the slots will also affect the draft feature of the escapement; this is a point which we should bear in mind whenever we make a change in the position of the pallet stones. The effect of moving the R stone out is to increase the draft on both stones, whereas if the L stone is moved out and the R stone in, it will decrease the draft. In order to ascertain that the escape wheel is correct, the lock and the drop should be tried with every tooth in the wheel on both pallet stones. This should be done with the bankings adjusted close, so as to just permit the teeth to drop. And the best way to try this, is to move the balance slowly with the finger while the pallet action is observed through the peepholes. After completing the adjustment of the pallet action the jewel pin action is next to be considered. The fork should swing an equal distance to each side of the centre line when the pallet is banked to drop. If we find that it moves farther on one side than the other, it will be necessary to bend the fork close to the pallet a sufficient amount to bring it in line. This is called "adjusting the let-off". The test for the let-off is to see that when the pallet is banked to drop, the jewel pin is just as close to the corner of the fork, in passing out, on one side as on the other. This test is correct, provided that the fork is of equal length on both sides of the slot, as it should be. The test for the fork length is that it should allow the jewel pin to pass out on both sides when the pallet is banked to drop. This is the maximum length which is allowed for the fork. The test for short fork is to move the balance so as to unlock the pallet, then reverse the motion and see that the pallet is carried back safely to lock by the jewel pin. This should be tried on both pallet stones. It is, however, customary to try the shake of the fork when the centre of the jewel pin is opposite the corner of the fork, and not to allow the pallet to unlock from this shake. In order to ensure perfect freedom in the jewel pin action, the jewel pin should be from ·01 to ·015 mm. smaller than the slot in the fork. The safety action is also adjusted, while the escapement is banked to drop. The guard pin should be made just barely free from the roller when the fork is against the banking, and this should be tried carefully on both sides. If this is done correctly, the roller will have the necessary clearance when the bankings are opened to allow for the slide.

The operation of moving a pallet stone is one that requires a great deal of experience before one is able to do it satisfactorily except by repeated trials. Special tools called "pallet warmers" have been devised for holding the pallet during this operation. In the simplest form this tool consists of a small metal plate, about as large as a 12-size barrel, with a wire handle by which it is held while it is heated. This plate should have one or more holes drilled in it as clearance for the pallet arbor. An improved form of this tool is shown in

Fig. 78A, page 60. The pallet is placed top-side down against this plate, and the whole of it is warmed over the alcohol flame until the shellac is softened so the stones can be moved.

A good way of applying shellac for the fastening of pallet stones is to warm some stick or button shellac, over a flame and pull it out in long threads of about ·5 mm. diameter. Shellac in this form is very convenient to use, as it is only necessary when the pallet is heated to the proper temperature, to touch the end of this thread to it at the place where the shellac is wanted. With a little practice one can learn to deposit just the right amount. After the pallet is cold all shellac on the surface should be cleaned off carefully with a scraper made of brass or nickel.

The Jewel Pin Action.—The fork and jewel pin action involves two distinct functions; the impulse and the unlocking. In order to illustrate and make this statement clear, we will consider the different parts of the escapement in a normal position, as shown on page 51, Fig. 75. The hairspring, controlling the balance, has brought the fork, by means of the jewel pin, to the normal position of rest.

This leaves the pallet in a position where the impulse face of an escape wheel tooth will engage the impulse face of one or the other of the pallet stones, in this instance the R stone. Assuming the parts to be in this relation to each other. it is evident that when power is applied to the escape wheel, the escape wheel tooth which is engaging the R stone will cause the pallet to turn on its pivots, and this impulse is transmitted to the balance by the fork acting on the jewel pin. The impulse being completed, the escape tooth drops off from the R stone, and the second tooth forward comes to lock on the L stone, with the fork resting against the banking, as shown on page 52, Fig. 76. The fork slot is now in such a position that the jewel pin may pass out perfectly free, and this condition is necessary because the impulse which was given to the balance imparted to that member a certain momentum, causing it to continue to turn in that direction until this momentum is overcome by the tension of the hairspring. During this part of the motion, which takes place after the impulse, the jewel pin leaves the fork entirely, but the instant that the momentum in the balance is overcome by the tension in the spring. the balance will start to turn in the opposite direction, the tendency of the spring being to bring the jewel pin to the centre line. Before reaching this point, however, the jewel pin has to perform the very important function of unlocking. At the completion of the impulse we left the fork resting on the banking, with the fork slot in such position that the jewel pin *passed out* perfectly freely, and, figuring on the assistance of the draft and safety action, which will be explained later, we are justified in expecting that the jewel pin shall *pass in* to the fork slot perfectly freely. The instant the jewel pin has entered the slot, and comes in contact with the fork, the work of unlocking begins. And here is to be noticed that for every tick of the watch, the pallet and fork is started from the condition of rest, by a sudden blow of the jewel pin. And not only the pallet is started, but the *whole train has to be started in the reverse direction*, against the power of the mainspring, to unlock the escape wheel in order to receive another impulse. The impulse on the L stone being completed, the pallet assumes the position shown on page 50. The jewel pin passing out on an excursion, the same as on the other side, returns to unlock, receives a new impulse, and so on, at the rate of 18,000 times per hour. In view of the above it is evident that lightness, as far as it is consistent with strength and wearing quality, is an essential feature in the construction of the several parts. It was once considered necessary to attach a counterweight to the pallet in order to get it in poise, but with the modern light construction of pallet and fork, it has been proven beyond a doubt that the ordinary form of counterpoise was worse than useless, inasmuch as it involved an added mass of metal whose inertia must be overcome at each vibration of the balance.

The Safety Action.—The function of the safety action is to guard the escapement against unlocking from sudden shocks, or outside influences, while the jewel pin is out of engagement with the fork. In the lower grades of watch movements this guard duty is assigned to the edge of the table roller and the guard pin. The passing hollow, a small cut in the edge of the roller, directly outside the jewel pin, allows the guard pin to pass the centre line during the jewel pin action. This form of safety action is called "single roller" and is shown in plan in Figs. 77 and 78, on page 53. As will be seen from this drawing, the edge of the roller is made straight, or cylindrical, and the guard pin is bent in such a way as to present a curved portion to the edge of the roller. The advantage gained from this construction is that the guard pin can be adjusted forward or back by simply bending it at the base, without its action being in any way affected by a reasonable amount of endwise movement of either the balance staff or the pallet arbor. The double roller escapement, Fig. 76, page 52, presents a more desirable form of safety action, for two reasons: first, the intersection of the guard pin with the roller is much greater, making it perfectly safe against catching or wedging; second, any shock, or jar, causing the guard pin to touch the roller, will have less effect on the running of the watch, because the impinging takes place on a smaller diameter. The diagrams, Figs. 77 and 78, illustrate the above statements. The wedge action of the guard pin, when it is brought to the roller, is represented by the lines C and D, which are at right-angles to

Fig. 78a.—A pallet warmer, for setting the pallet stones.

the lines A and B, thus forming tangents to the points of contact. It will be seen that with the single roller this wedge is 17°, whereas in the double roller it is 30°, a very considerable difference in favour of the double roller.

Directions for Putting the Escapement in Beat.—An escapement is said to be in beat when it requires the same amount of power to start the balance in one direction as in the other. This should be tried with the mainspring only partly wound up, by arresting the motion of the balance with a pointed object held between the heads of two balance screws, and allowing the balance to move slowly, first in one direction and then in the other. If it appears to require more power in order to let off on one side than the other, it is said to be "out of beat", and it should be corrected by turning the hairspring collet a certain amount, on the balance staff, until it takes the same amount of power to let off on one pallet stone as on the other. This is usually done without removing the balance, by reaching in over the top side of the hairspring with a special tool made of small steel wire and flattened at the end so as to enter the slot in the collet. Great care should, however, be exercised in doing this work, so as to avoid bending the hairspring out of true.

CHAPTER VI

THE CYLINDER ESCAPEMENT

THE cylinder escapement must not be despised even though it is not to be found in the high-grade watch. This type of escapement is still popular with the cheaper movement where it often gives a considerably better performance than some lever escapements.

As its name implies, the main unit of this escapement consists of a cylinder. The pivoted cylinder, to which is attached the balance wheel, occupies the same place as the balance staff in the lever escapement. The escape wheel, which is of peculiar design, works directly into the cylinder; there is no intermediate connection like the lever or pallets. Brass escape wheels and jewelled cylinders were used by the early makers, but the best results have been obtained by using steel wheels and cylinders.

Unlike the lever, which is a detached escapement, the cylinder is essentially frictional, for the escape wheel teeth rub the edge of the cylinder for a considerable part of the balance vibration. Fig. 82 shows the escape wheel and cylinder, From the sketch it will be seen that the teeth are mounted upon stalks, whilst the plan view reveals the wedge-shaped tooth.

In the action of the escapement, a point of an escape wheel tooth rests on the outside of the cylinder, and as the balance revolves, the tooth forces its way into the cylinder, at the same time giving impulse to the balance. The cylinder, which is, of course, cut away to allow the teeth to enter, now receives the tooth on its inside. There is a little drop as the heel of the tooth leaves the lip of the cylinder.

The tooth remains inside the cylinder until the balance reaches the end of its vibration. When the balance returns it allows the tooth inside the cylinder to escape, and the point of the next tooth to drop on to the outside of the cylinder. In a cylinder escapement, the banking is provided by the balance and the balance bridge. A short pin is fitted into the edge of the balance wheel whilst the banking stud usually consists of a pin attached to the underside of the bridge. Unless the banking stud is close to the rim of the wheel, excessive vibration is likely to cause the banking pin to lock itself on the banking stud.

c

THE CYLINDER ESCAPEMENT

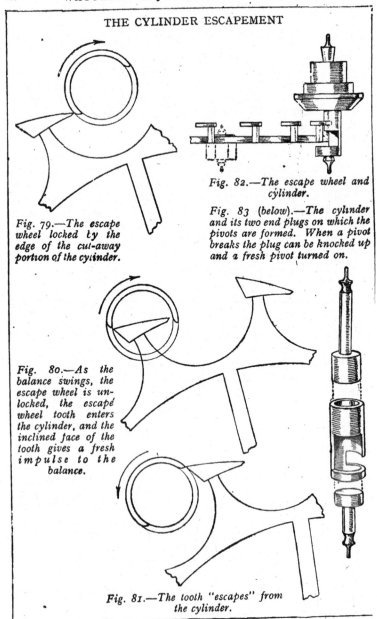

Fig. 79.—*The escape wheel locked by the edge of the cut-away portion of the cylinder.*

Fig. 82.—*The escape wheel and cylinder.*

Fig. 83 (below).—*The cylinder and its two end plugs on which the pivots are formed. When a pivot breaks the plug can be knocked up and a fresh pivot turned on.*

Fig. 80.—*As the balance swings, the escape wheel is unlocked, the escape wheel tooth enters the cylinder, and the inclined face of the tooth gives a fresh impulse to the balance.*

Fig. 81.—*The tooth "escapes" from the cylinder.*

High quality escapements are provided with a series of dots to assist in setting the balance in beat. Three dots on the bottom plate and one dot on the balance. When the balance is at rest, its dot should be opposite the middle dot. To test the beat, turn the balance until a tooth drops, note the position of the balance dot in relation to one of the outer dots. Reverse the balance and note its position. If the dots coincide or bear the same relative position to each other, the escapement will be in beat. If the positions are unequal, the hairspring will have to be moved until they become equal.

Should the escape wheel have drop outside the cylinder, but no drop inside the cylinder will be too small, if the conditions are reversed the cylinder will be too large. These faults can only be remedied by fitting a new cylinder. Unequal escape wheel teeth can be equalised by filing the tips of the teeth with a diamond file. The lower cylinder jewel is carried in a movable brass bar called the chariot. In high-class watches this is a separate bar carrying a jewel and an end-piece fixed by a screw or screws. Cheap mass-produced watches have the bottom plate pierced to allow movement to be made, a clumsy but effective method.

By moving the chariot the engagement of the escape wheel with the cylinder can be made deeper or shallower. If the depth is shallow, the balance will trip, and, if the watch continues to go, it will naturally gain considerably. Frequently, the underside of the escape wheel rubs the base of the cylinder opening. To give a clear passage, lay the escape on a hollow brass stake, select a hollow steel punch a little smaller than the rim of the wheel, and stretch the arms of the wheel upwards by delivering one or two light blows with a hammer. Should the lower edge of the cylinder opening rub the upper of the escape wheel, the wheel should be laid upside down on the stake and stretched upwards as previously described.

CHAPTER VII

DISMANTLING: FITTING WINDING SHAFTS

As soon as a watch comes in for repair it should be thoroughly examined. It is a good plan to ask the owner a few questions about the past history of the watch. Answers to such questions as "Has it kept time in all positions?" "Have you had a new mainspring fitted recently?" will help towards a quicker diagnosis.

Before opening the bezel, examine the glass, which should be a perfectly tight fit. Frequently the bezel is fitted with an unsuitable glass. If the bezel is one with only a narrow inner flange to keep it away from the dial it will need a higher glass than one with a deep inner flange. Fig. 84 shows various kinds of watch glass.

Glasses.—It is surprising how many glasses carry a circular scratch made by the minute hand. Usually this indicates a low glass. By placing the nail upon the glass above the minute hand some idea can be gathered of the distance between the hand and the glass. If the watch is not working the ear test is quite effective. Pull out the winder to the set hands position, place the glass close to the ear and turn the winder. A light scraping noise will be heard if the hand is touching the glass. With small watches this test may not be effective, so something more positive is necessary. Mix a spot of rouge with a spot of oil and apply it to the highest point of the minute hand, snap down the bezel, and set the hands. Open the bezel and examine the glass. If there is a red ring it will prove that the hand is too high. The hands should be both parallel to each other and to the dial in all positions.

Thin Cases.—Modern cases are tragically thin. They should be carefully inspected for broken hinges, cracks, torn loops and last but not least tiny pin-holes in the bezel. Mirage and other fancy shaped bezels having a number of sharp corners give endless trouble in this way. The holes are often very minute, but they allow a considerable amount of dust to enter, and unless they are covered it is useless to clean the movement. The easiest way to fill the holes is to remove the glass, apply a little flux and a tiny piece of soft or tinman's solder at each hole and gently warm the bezel over a low gas or spirit flame.

Well oil the hinge before warming the bezel for the heat may affect its action.

The winding button and shaft should also receive attention. If this is worn, there will be plenty of room for dirt and dust to enter through the shaft hole. As well as the possibility of losing the complete winder undue strain will be placed upon

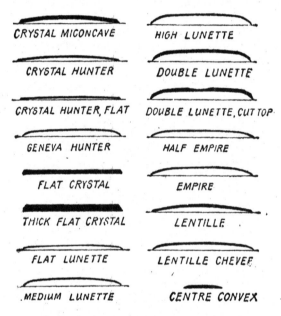

CRYSTAL MICONCAVE

HIGH LUNETTE

CRYSTAL HUNTER

DOUBLE LUNETTE

CRYSTAL HUNTER, FLAT

DOUBLE LUNETTE, CUT TOP

GENEVA HUNTER

HALF EMPIRE

FLAT CRYSTAL

EMPIRE

THICK FLAT CRYSTAL

LENTILLE

FLAT LUNETTE

LENTILLE CHEVEE

MEDIUM LUNETTE

CENTRE CONVEX

Fig. 84.—Various types of watch-glasses.

the shaft and the internal winding operation and hand setting mechanism. Continuous operation of the winder in this condition will finally end in a breakage. If the wear is excessive a new oversize shaft will be necessary. First remove the dial by unscrewing the dial feet screws. In some watches the screws are placed in the edge of the bottom plate and only accessible when the movement has been removed from the case. In others, the screws are provided with a semi-circular flange at the base and screwed into the top surface of the bottom plate. If the minute hand is a good fit take care in levering it off, otherwise it may jump away. If the "seconds" hand is a tight fit, carefully raise the dial which will also act

as a lever and remove the hand.   The hour hand will come away
with the dial, bringing with it the hour wheel.

Dismantling the Works.—When the dial has been removed
unscrew the cover piece which keeps the spring return lever—
a small lever working in the groove of the castle wheel—and
the hand-setting wheel in place, remove the castle and crown
wheels, and everything is ready for fitting the new winding
shaft.   Fig. 85 shows the crown wheel, and castle wheel.
Select a "rough"—in other words a partly finished winding
shaft—that is a little larger than the hole between the plates,
as most of the wear will have taken place here and in the pivot
hole.   With the old shaft as a pattern mark off the length to
the end of the pivot.   Place the shaft in a suitable lathe chuck

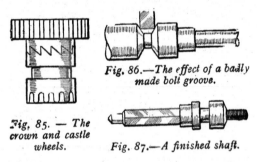

Fig. 85. — The
crown and castle
wheels.

Fig. 86.—The effect of a badly
made bolt groove.

Fig. 87.—A finished shaft.

and turn down the shoulder and the pivot.   When the new
shaft has been turned down a little try the fit.   To do this
there is no need to remove the shaft from the chuck, simply
take the plates to the shaft and there will be every opportunity
of making a moderately tight fit.   Leave the shaft a little tight
to turn as final buffing will reduce it to a smooth action.

The Crown Wheel.—As the squared part of the shaft is
always smaller than the shoulder for the crown wheel it will be
quite safe to mark the position of the crown wheel shoulder
and turn the shaft down until it just fits the crown wheel.
When the shaft has been turned to fit the crown wheel,
remove it from the lathe chuck and place it in a hand chuck.
It is most important that the squared section should be square.
Failure to do this may cause the castle wheel to have an
uncertain action.   Most watchmakers use a boxwood block for
filing purposes—a small cube of box wood.   Although box is
a hard wood, steel pieces will become firmly embedded.

If you feel a little uncertain with regard to your filing

capabilities, reverse the crown wheel and place it upon the shaft. It will act as a guide and prevent filing the crown wheel shoulder. Use a fine file with a safety edge. Try the castle wheel on each square to make sure the action is smooth. When the square is finished replace the winding wheels in the watch, and put the shaft in place and try the forward and backward action. Lightly screw up the pull-up or bolt piece which retains the shaft, and mark the position of the slot. Care should be taken in making the sides of the slot straight as a V-shaped slot will be inclined to force the bolt out. Fig. 86 shows the effect of a badly made slot.

Sharp Corners.—Whilst the shaft is still in the lathe turn the pivot to a point as this will make entry easier. The corners of the lower end of the square can be turned off too. Sharp corners have a nasty habit of cutting away the brass plate and upsetting the winding. Put the winding shaft in place and screw the bolt piece tight. Mark off the position of the end of the shaft a little beyond the pendant—the tubular extension on the side of the case—remove the shaft and cut it off. Always remove a shaft before cutting it off, as the shock is quite sufficient to break a balance pivot. If the end is already screwed, attach the winding button. If the end is plain turn it down to a suitable size for threading. Fig. 87 shows a finished shaft.

Interchangeable shafts are supplied by the material dealers for most of the modern watches. If ordering by post, the size of the movement and the make, or preferably the broken part of the old shaft if available, should be sent to the dealer.

CHAPTER VIII

FITTING MAINSPRINGS

ALTHOUGH the mainspring is a very essential part of a watch, it is frequently treated by repairers as though it were of a minor rather than a major importance. The life of a mainspring is by no means everlasting. In fact, many mainsprings have a decidedly short life. This makes it all the more difficult to convince a watch owner that a new mainspring is necessary when the watch is working with the existing mainspring.

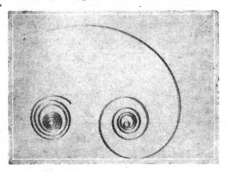

Fig. 88.—Showing an old and new spring. That on the left has been in use for a considerable time.

Removing a Spring.—When a mainspring is run down there should be as much unoccupied space as the spring occupies when it is lying against the side of the barrel. The space in the barrel should be allotted equally to the mainspring, the barrel arbor and the unoccupied space—one-third each. When removing a spring from a barrel, pull up the inner coil carefully and allow the spring slowly to unwind itself from the barrel against your fingers. To let the spring literally fly out from the barrel will be courting disaster, as the necessary entanglement of the coils will distort the spring and render it useless. Loss of power is often difficult to discover when it is not constant. It is very important therefore to make a careful examination of the spring when it has been removed.

The appearance of bright spots will indicate friction between the coils with a consequent jerky or unequal pull. Oil will have little effect upon coil friction, and the balance action will be certain to "fall off" at the weak pull. The only remedy will be a new mainspring. If there are bright marks on the edge of the spring, and the barrel cover shows a series of circular scratches, this will indicate that the spring is fouling the cover, a frequent cause of loss of power. One remedy is to reduce the thickness of the barrel cover by placing it in a lathe step chuck and turning off some of the excess metal, taking care not to remove any of the arbor bearing in the operation. If the cover is too thin to reduce, a new spring, a size lower, will have to be fitted.

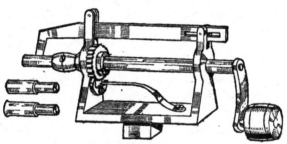

Fig. 89.—A popular mainspring winder.

Faulty Mainspring.—The fact that a watch goes does not signify that it is going correctly. The escapement and all the other parts may be in perfect adjustment, but still the balance may not have the action it should. In this case the fault can usually be traced to the mainspring. The coils should not be disturbed any more than is absolutely necessary, which probably accounts for this attitude of indifference towards the mainspring. If the coils are very gummy the spring should be soaked in benzine, and then allowed to dry off. Any slight stickiness can be removed by passing a piece of folded tissue paper between the coils with the aid of a pair of tweezers.

Fig. 88 is an actual photograph of two mainsprings (an old spring and a new spring). That on the left has been in use for a considerable time, and has become "dead" in the centre. In other words the inner coils have lost a good deal of their elasticity. If this spring were fully wound it would probably give the balance a fair action for the first 12 hours; but after that there would be a considerable "falling off" in the action, which would seriously affect the timekeeping. Such a spring is really unfit for further use.

The Barrel Arbor.—The barrel arbor should be a good fit in both barrel and cover, with only the minimum of endshake. As the mainspring exerts a certain amount of twisting force when wound, an ill-fitting barrel will also be inclined to twist and undoubtedly come into contact with the underside of the centre wheel with disastrous results. If either of the holes need re-bushing, broach or reamer the hole round, turn a small stopping of brass or nickel and rivet it in position. Place the barrel or cover in a step chuck, turn off any surplus rivet, centre the new bush and drill a true hole. Finally broach the hole to fit the arbor and chamfer a small oil sink.

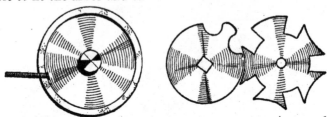

Figs. 90 & 91.—A new hook before being cut off. (Right).—The stop work mechanism to prevent overwinding, and also to ensure that the spring does not run down beyond a certain point, thus making for better timekeeping, and even tension throughout the 24 hours.

The safety of the mainspring depends upon a good hooking attachment. If the barrel hook is one of the screwed or riveted type, it should be perfectly rigid. It should never stand out from one side of the barrel more than the thickness of the spring. The smaller the hook the better; a large hook will not only be more difficult to fix, but it will occupy more space in the barrel. To fit a new hook, drill and tap a small hole through the side of the barrel at an angle. This will give a longer hole and allow more threads.

File a piece of steel wire and tap it until it shows a full thread, cut off a little above the full thread, and file the top and two sides flat. Screw the new hook from the inside to the outside until only the head stands out from the side of the barrel, cut off the surplus and file flat (Fig. 90). It will be an advantage to undercut the hooking side of the head with a slitting file.

The Barrel Hook.—Modern watches favour the recessed type of barrel hook—a step cut in the side of the barrel—as there is no risk of undue projection. As this kind of hook is very shallow it must be square cut to prevent the mainspring from slipping. Any sign of a rounded nose can be rectified by using a sharp, long-pointed graver. Many barrels have a hook which has been pressed through the side with a special tool, and many mainspring punches have a cutter for this purpose, but the risk of distorting the barrel with one of these punches is so great that the screwed-in hook is a much better proposition.

Types of Spring.—When replacing a worn or broken mainspring it should not be assumed that the existing spring is the original or even the correct kind of spring for the watch. It may be too weak or too strong. With a strong spring the balance would have an excessive vibration when fully wound with a sudden decline after a few hours, whilst at the end of 24 hours running the balance would probably come to rest if

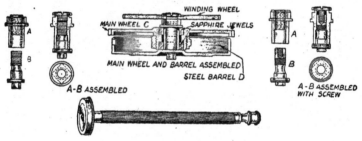

Fig. 92.—The Waltham mainspring barrel. It is of the "free" type. Below, the special tool for separating the barrel.

the watch was placed in a "pendant" up position. Such a condition is most undesirable. A weaker spring would give a smaller but more constant vibration and serve the same purpose as a stop work. The purpose of a stop work, which consists of a finger-piece attached to the barrel arbor engaging with a star wheel screwed to the barrel or barrel covers, is to allow only the middle turns of the mainspring to be used.

The stop-work allows only four turns, so that a spring which makes six turns will permit the stop-work being set up one complete turn, and still allow one turn unused. Fig. 91 shows a stop-work mechanism. From this it will be gathered that at least four turns of spring are necessary. At least five turns should be aimed at whether or not the watch is fitted with a stop-work, as this will give a little reserve. When the length of spring has been determined the outside end will have to be fitted with a hook according to the type of barrel. If a stop-work is fitted, an ordinary hole will be quite suitable, as the spring will never be pulled completely away from the side of the barrel. Before punching or drilling the hole remove the excess hardness from the end of the spring by "letting it down" over a spirit flame. Run a broach through at an angle to make a sharp hooking edge, file the end round and finish with an emery buff. Watches not fitted with a stop-work need a more resilient form of hooking as the mainspring is pulled well away from the side of the barrel when fully wound.

Pivoted Brace Hook.—Many pocket watches use the pivoted brace hook. This consists of a small tongue with two pivots,

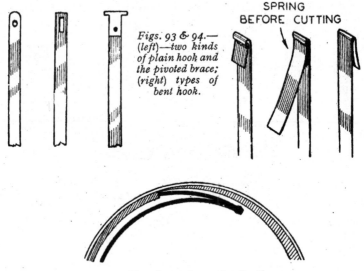

Figs. 93 & 94.— (left)—two kinds of plain hook and the pivoted brace; (right) types of bent hook.

SPRING BEFORE CUTTING

Fig. 95.—How the spring end grips the recess in the mainspring barrel.

riveted to the end of the spring. The pivots fit in holes drilled in the cover and bottom of the barrel. The pivoted brace allows the spring to be tightly wound without undue strain on the extreme end. When fitting a pivoted brace hook make sure that it does not exceed the width of the spring, or what is probably worse, be out of alignment with the spring. Fig. 93 shows two kinds of plain hook and the pivoted brace.

Plain Bent Overhook.—Quite 50 per cent of the mainsprings fitted by the manufacturers have a plain bent overhook, made by heating the end of the spring, doubling it back and squeezing it flat with a pair of pliers. Although the manufacturers use this kind of hook it is not one of the best. There is too much strain at the actual bend. Ample proof is to be found in the number of springs which break at this particular point. A much more satisfactory hook is one in which a loose piece of spring is inserted between the bent end of the mainspring and the barrel. To make a hook, gently warm the spring at the point at which it is to be bent (the waste part will bend itself back). As the spring becomes red, squeeze it gently with a pair of pliers. Break off a small piece of waste spring, place it between the bend, warm the end again until it becomes red and squeeze tightly. The squeezing must be done whilst the spring is red, or there will be a tendency to break.

When cold, cut off the waste spring, using the edge of a triangular or square file to make the cut, leaving just a small bend. File off the corners and buff off the discoloured part of

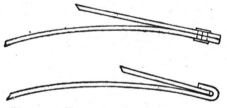

Fig. 95a.—Two types of mainspring end— the riveted and the loose end.

the spring. Cut off another small piece of waste spring (there are usually 2 or 3 inches to spare) and insert it in the hook. Fig. 94 shows types of bent hook. Fingers should never be used to wind a spring into a barrel. Apart from finger-marking, which is likely to lead to rust, the spring will assume a spiral shape causing friction with the barrel cover and a consequent loss of power. Wind the spring on the mainspring winder arbor first, place the barrel over the spring, reverse the ratchet on the winder and let the spring unwind itself into the barrel. Fig. 89 shows a popular mainspring winder.

Special springs and springs with patent hooking devices should be specially obtained. In fact, the spring designed by the makers should be used whenever possible, as it will provide the maximum of power.

CHAPTER IX

CLEANING A WATCH

AFTER the movement is taken apart remove the balance jewels, and also the escape and pallet arbor jewels (if these parts are cap jewelled). Before taking these out, however, we should see if the settings of the hole jewels are marked for position, and if they are not marked, we should make a small dot near the edge of each setting so they can be replaced correctly after the cleaning. The following is the order in which these settings are marked in Waltham movements. In the lower plate they are marked as shown in the illustration.

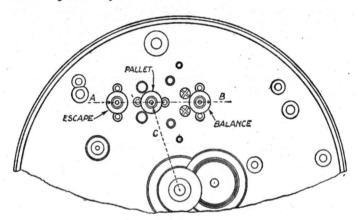

Fig. 96.—Back plate of a Waltham pocket watch, showing how the jewels are marked. They must be replaced in that position.

The balance and the escape jewels on the sides away from the pallet, and the pallet arbor jewel on the side towards the centre of the movement. In the top plate all the jewels are marked on the side towards the centre of the movement. After this has been attended to put all the parts (except the balance) in benzine, to remove oil and greasy matter. After the oil is cleaned off string a few pieces at a time on a wire loop, or hook, as shown in Fig. 97, page 75, and wash in hot water with a medium soft brush and Castile soap. While the parts are on

Fig. 97.—Method of suspending the plate in the cyanide solution.

the hook, dip in a solution of cyanide of potassium (see directions for making, page 78) for one or two seconds; rinse thoroughly in clean water, immerse in alcohol for about 10 seconds, and dry in warm boxwood sawdust. When the mainspring is taken out of the barrel it should be handled carefully, and no attempt made to straighten it out. If the oil on it appears gummy it should be cleaned off thoroughly with benzine, but if the oil appears good it is better to only wipe the spring with a piece of cloth by folding it around the spring and sliding it along without straightening the spring. After the spring is put back in the barrel, which, by the way, should be done with a good mainspring winder, it should be oiled with good quality watch oil in sufficient quantity to ensure thorough lubrication without risk of spreading on the outside of the barrel.

The escapement jewels, after going through the benzine, should be taken, one at a time, with a pair of specially prepared tweezers, to avoid their snapping away, and held against a flat board, or a large piece of cork, and brushed thoroughly, one side at a time, with a fine toothbrush dipped in alcohol. After the brushing dip the jewel in clean alcohol, and dry between linen cloths.

After going through this process, we are reasonably sure that the jewels are clean, but I recommend, to make absolutely sure, a careful rubbing with a piece of peg-wood,

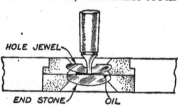

HOLE JEWEL

END STONE   OIL

Fig. 98.—Capillary attraction keeps the oil in place.

which has been pointed so as to go through the holes, and also one which is specially shaped for rubbing the cups in the jewels. After the jewels and endstones are put back in the plates, but before the movement is put up, the cap jewelled holes should be oiled. This is an operation which should be done with utmost care, as it is very important to give the right quantity of oil. The consequence of too much oil at these points is almost as bad as lack of oil. For the purpose of retaining a sufficient amount of oil in the pivot holes, we take advantage of a natural phenomena which is called capillary action. This action is, roughly stated, the tendency of liquids to run in between surfaces which are nearly in contact, and also to run upwards quite rapidly in very small tubes against the force of gravity.

The capillary action is strikingly illustrated in the wick of a lamp in which the close proximity of the fibres to each other, acting like capillary tubes, causes the oil to run upwards through the wick as fast as it burns at the top end of it. In view of these facts, and by the aid of Fig. 98 on page 75 I shall endeavour to explain why sometimes a pivot will run dry in a short time because we gave too much oil in the pivot hole. Looking at the drawing we find that the hole jewel is convex on the side towards the endstone, and also that there is a certain distance between the two jewels. This space is usually made about ·02 to ·03 mm., and is for the purpose of providing a reservoir for the oil.

And the convex shape of the hole jewel tends to keep the oil around the pivot, being attracted by the close space nearest the hole, by virtue of the capillary action referred to above. Now if we should give so much oil that it would fill the space to the edge of the hole jewel, it would immediately be attracted by the close space between the settings, which would pull it away and leave the pivot without a reserve supply of oil. The oil between the jewels ought to show in the proportion indicated on the drawing, or nearly so. For applying the oil we recommend an oiler made of small wire, about ·40 mm. diameter, preferably gold, which is filed tapering almost to a point, and the end flattened by hammering. This flattened point will hold the oil in a fairly definite quantity, so we know how much we deposit in the hole. After the oil has been put in the cup of the jewel, if it does not run down, we should coax it to do so by inserting the point of a pivot broach, and not consider the job done until we know by inspection that the oil has filled in properly between the jewels.

The cleaning of the balance with the hairspring requires special care, as it cannot be brushed safely. The usual method is to put it on a hook and dip it for a few seconds, first in water, then in cyanide; rinse in water, dip in alcohol and dry carefully in sawdust. The balance may be buffed afterwards with a string of chamois skin held in a wire bow, to brighten the rim, as well as the screws. After the balance has been cleaned, it should be examined carefully for any minute fibre that might have caught in the balance screws, or particles of sawdust in the slots of the screw heads. When cleaning a balance, if the jewel pin is set with shellac, and also when cleaning pallets, care must be taken not to leave them in the alcohol very long, as it would dissolve the shellac and loosen the jewels.

After the movement is set up the remainder of the pivots should be oiled and also the pallet stones or the escape wheel

*Fig. 99.—A wooden setting-up block for
re-assembling the movement after cleaning.*

teeth. But *do not oil the jewel pin* or the safety action. In the stem winding work all the bearing surfaces should be oiled, including the square of the winding arbor where it runs through the clutch. Here it may be well to emphasize the importance of taking good care of the oil which we use. It should be kept in a dark and cool place, and we should put only a drop or two at a time in our oil cup. A small agate cup with boxwood cover, such as is furnished by dealers in watch tools, is best adapted for use on the bench. This should always be cleaned before putting in fresh oil, and covered when it is not in use to prevent contamination of the oil by dust, etc.

The setting up of a full plate movement is often found

difficult for a beginner, on account of the potence into which
the fork must project. The Waltham Full Plate Movement,
18-size (a popular watch) is set up most conveniently on its
pillar plate, by leaving out the pallet and fork until after we put
on the top plate, and raising the top plate on the pallet side,
allowing it to rock on the two pillars on each side of the barrel,
a sufficient amount to give room for inserting the pallet and
fork. The setting up of a later pattern Waltham 18-size movement, should be done *on its top plate* by using a block like

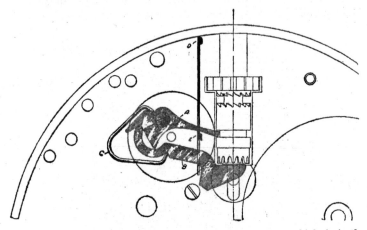

Fig. 100.—*The Waltham pendant setting mechanism in which* A *is the
shipper,* B *the shipper lever, and* C *the shipper spring. They are shown
in the normal position (movement out of case), in the hand-setting position.
This setting mechanism is known as " negative set", and it is used in
conjunction with a pendant device shown in Figs. 103 and 104.*

the one shown in Fig. 99, for holding the plate. The opposite
side of this block is made to fit the pillar plate after the
movement is turned over for inserting the plate screws. This
block is supplied to watchmakers by the Waltham Watch
Company, free of charge, on application.

The best kind of alcohol for cleaning watch parts is commercial grain alcohol. I would not recommend using either
denatured or wood alcohol for this purpose.

The cyanide solution referred to should be made in the
proportion of 7 ounces, avoirdupois, to 1 gallon of water, and
this solution should be renewed as soon as it shows a tendency
to turn dark. *Cyanide of Potassium is a virulent poison*, and

great care must be taken in handling it. It is considered deadly if reaching an open scratch in the skin. The fumes should also be avoided. A good way for keeping both the

Fig. 101.—The recoiling click in the lifting position during winding.

Fig. 102.—The recoiling click in the "lock" position after winding. When the spring is fully wound the click recoils and thus prevents overwinding.

cyanide and alcohol for cleaning watches is in 1 gallon specimen or candy jars, with ground glass covers, and marked with *conspicuous warning labels.*

Casing.—Before putting a watch movement in its case always oil the winding bar in the pendant, where it runs in the sleeve, to prevent rust and squeaking. See that the movement lines up properly with the winding bar in the case, so it will wind and back ratchet freely. It is sometimes necessary to remove the winding bar and sleeve from the case pendant and enlarge the hole in it to one side or the other, with a round file, in order to get a perfectly free action. The length of the square on the winding bar should also be looked after to see that both the winding and setting action is right. If the square is too

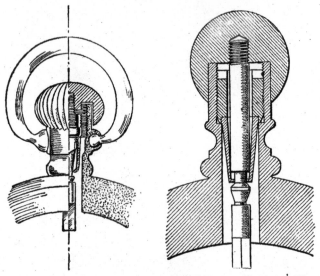

Figs. 103 & 104.—*The pendant set or negative set mechanism. The split sleeve acts as a lock and retains the mechanism in the winding position. When the button is pulled the coned portion of the winding shaft opens the sleeve and locks the mechanism in the set-hands position.*

long it may be shortened by filing without removing it from the case. If it is too short it is necessary to remove the crown and turn in the sleeve nut until the action is right. See that the crystal does not touch the centre, and that the hands clear the dial and the crystal, as well as each other. After the case is closed hold the watch to your ear and listen if the balance pivots will "bump" clear on both endstones, as they should do, when the watch is tipped from side to side. This will indicate if the case in any way interferes with the freedom of the balance.

CHAPTER X

FURTHER NOTES ON CLEANING

LET us consider the subject of cleaning in detail. After an external examination the movement should be dismantled and subjected to a further examination. It is not a good policy to clean and polish the movement if it has to be handled afterwards for the purpose of effecting repairs and adjustments. On the other hand it is impossible to ascertain whether repairs are necessary if the parts are coated with a black greasy paste.

Before letting down the mainspring a note should be made of any unusual features and adjustments necessary. After letting down the mainspring remove the various components which should be placed in a movement tray or a small box. Wine glasses, from which the stems have been accidentally broken, make excellent dust covers and are to be found on many watchmakers' benches. Separating the parts will prevent a mix-up of the screws, many of which are of different lengths. Movements in different states of dirtiness require different methods of cleaning. If the movement is comparatively new and has only stopped because of dust, dry brushing will be effective.

First wipe the plates with a chamois leather; afterwards hold them in tissue paper and brush them with a circular motion. Brushing in any other way will produce unsightly scratches which can only be removed by re-gilding. For ease and speed the tissue paper should be cut into small squares about 4 × 3 inches, and hung in a convenient place. Several brushes should be in use at the same time. A small brush is very useful when dealing with miniature watches. When in use a brush should be constantly rubbed on a block of specially prepared chalk. This chalk is sold for the purpose of keeping watch brushes clean. A periodical washing in lukewarm water will prolong the life of any brush.

When the plates have been brushed they should be carefully examined and the various wheel sinks and jewel sinks pegged free of any dirt which may have adhered to their rough edges. Pegwood, usually supplied in bundles of 25 sticks, is frequently called dogwood. Jewel holes should be thoroughly cleaned by twirling pegwood dipped in alcohol. The pegwood, which

should be sharpened with small facets to aid polishing, should
be repeatedly sharpened until it is withdrawn perfectly clean.

Many beginners pay too much
attention to outward finish and insufficient to jewel holes, pinions and
pivots. Pinion leaves, like jewel
holes, must be thoroughly pegged
after brushing. Pivots too
must be individually cleaned.
For small pivots twirl a piece
of pith well down to the
shoulder, for large pivots use
a piece of clean cork. The
ruby pin should be cleaned
with pith whilst the fork
should be cleaned with pegwood.

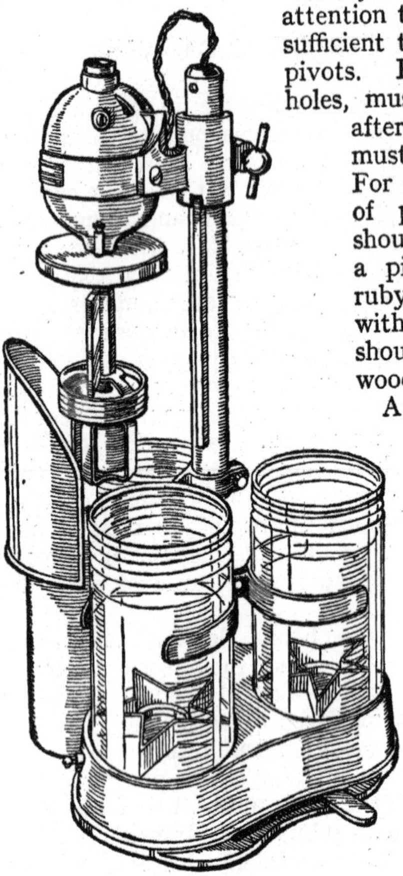

A point which is often over-
looked and one which
can have a retarding
effect upon the balance
is the cleanliness of the
banking pins. If there
is any doubt about the
cleanliness of these pins
and the sides of the
lever with which they
make contact, they
should be very lightly
scraped. Capped jewels,
that is jewel holes fitted
with endstones, must
be separated in order
that they may be scru-
pulously clean. Oil

Fig. 105.—A typical watch-cleaning machine. which remains in the
minute space between
jewel hole and endstone often becomes congealed. If this is
allowed to remain the clean oil will be contaminated.

A movement which is greasy will not respond to the dry brush
method. It will be necessary to immerse it (when dismantled)
in some cleansing solution such as very light benzine. For
final cleansing the parts can be dipped in alcohol. Pallet

stones and ruby pin must be closely watched as the alcohol is likely to dissolve the shellac by which they are fixed. After removal from the solution the parts should be dried in box-wood sawdust. When dry the pinions, jewel holes, etc., must be pegged. Great care must be taken to see that no speck of box-dust remains anywhere. One speck of box-dust, left under a balance screw or left in the slit of a balance screw, is sufficient to upset the time of a sensitive watch.

Care must be exercised when brushing delicate steel pieces as the slightest kinking can cause hours of labour when re-assembling the movement. Straight pieces should be brushed lengthwise whilst holding the piece carefully on the bench. A dusty balance and balance spring may be cleaned by stroking it with a camel-hair brush with a circular movement.

Watchmakers who were trained in the hand and brush method of cleaning are fast being converted to the mechanical method. The electrical watch-cleaning machine is now an essential item of the modern repair department. Although some of the old school are inclined to frown upon this invention, its efficiency cannot be disputed. There are several types of machine, but the principle is the same. The watch parts are cleaned by fluid friction. Unlike hand-brushing, in which the parts are held in tissue paper or the fingers, the mechanical cleaner leaves no finger marks.

The machine consists of an electric motor attached to a basket into which the parts of the watch are placed, jars of cleaning and rinsing solutions and a drying element. The watch is dismantled in the usual way and the parts placed in the basket—large parts in the bottom section, small parts in the top. The basket is lowered into No. 1 jar. The motor is started and the basket revolved for about a minute, the basket then being raised free of the liquid and any surplus thrown off.

Automatic sealing of the jars prevents any waste of solution. When removed from No. 1 jar the basket is placed in No. 2 jar and finally in No. 3 jar. Surplus solution should be thrown off each time. After the last rinse the basket should be rotated above the heater element and the parts dried. There is no likelihood of the parts being scratched as centrifugal action holds the parts against the wire basket. The basket should be rotated for about one minute in each solution.

Excessive speed should be avoided for although the basket may appear to be covered with solution, this is no guarantee

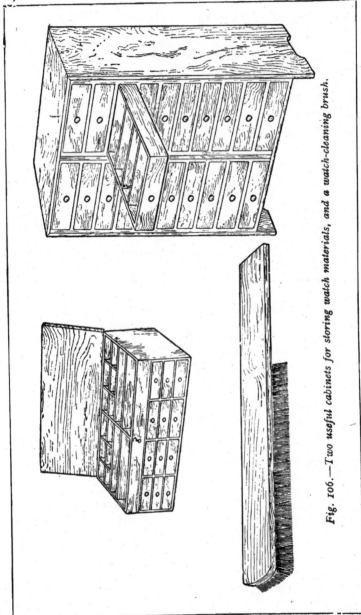

Fig. 106.—Two useful cabinets for storing watch materials, and a watch-cleaning brush.

that the parts inside are well covered. It is also important that any surplus solution should be thrown off, for any which remains is likely to contaminate the rinsing solution. No time should be lost in transferring from one solution to another. Failure in this operation may result in spotted plates or even rusty hairspring coils. Certain conditions cause some rinsing solutions to decompose. These solutions should never be left in strong sunlight.

When re-assembling the movement the parts should be held in tissue paper. A movement holder is very useful for miniature movements. Care should be taken not to breathe on the parts as condensation is likely to cause rust. A customer who quite casually blew into his watch to remove the dust was very disappointed when told it was full of rust.

A number of different-sized screwdrivers are essential if the brand new appearance of the watch is to be maintained. The screwdriver should be the same width as the screw. Too large a screwdriver will cause the screw sinks to be mutilated. A screwdriver blade with insufficient taper or too narrow will be inclined to slip out of the slit and damage the screw head.

Oiling a watch sounds a simple matter, but in order that the watch shall gain full benefit from the oil, it needs to be applied carefully. A considerable amount of research work has been carried out in recent years with the result that watch oils are now produced in a highly refined state. There are two kinds of oil—mineral and animal or vegetable. Although animal or vegetable oil does not spread it has the disadvantage of thickening. Mineral oils remain fresh but have a tendency to spread.

The introduction of the "Epilame" process has enabled mineral oil to be used. The treatment of the parts with "Epilame" prevents oil from spreading and helps it to form beads at the ends of pivots. One method of applying the "Epilame" is to immerse the parts in the solution so that the whole surface is covered with a most minute film. Another method is to place a little "Epilame" in a bottle with a pith stopper. The pith can be saturated and the pivots pushed into the pith. Sufficient "Epilame" can be applied with a sharpened piece of pegwood for the jewel holes. Note: "Epilame" must not be placed on mainsprings or pallet stones. To make the best use of this process, special oils are prepared and graded in conjunction with it.

For the actual application of the oil, some repairers use a pivot drill, others an ordinary steel pen. A good oiler can be made in the following manner. Cut off a piece of brass bush wire about three inches long. At one end fix a collar to prevent the end of the oiler touching the bench. A brass hexagonal nut soldered to the end will also prevent the oiler from rolling off the bench. The oiler proper can be filed from a needle or piece of steel wire. Fig. 107 shows an oiler.

When oiling balance and other capped jewels, it is important that the oil reaches the endstone. If the oil remains in the

Fig. 107.—Above, a watch oiler, so balanced that its point is prevented from touching the bench and so picking up grit; and (left) an oil-pot and cover.

reservoir of the jewel hole it will probably spread to the lower end of the roller or towards the hairspring collet. To enable the oil to reach the endstone use another oiler in which the steel part is filed small enough to enter the jewel hole thereby permitting the oil to follow through.

In small watches the most difficult part to oil is the top pallet pivot. The easiest way is to apply a spot of oil to the pivot before letting down the pallet bridge. The pallet staff shoulder is so short that more than the tiniest spot of oil is likely to spread and retard the action. Under ordinary circumstances a watch will run for twelve months before the need for further oil.

CHAPTER XI

CORRECTING A BALANCE AND PIVOTING

ONE of the most common breakages in a watch, apart from the main spring, is a broken balance staff. In some instances a fall or blow is sufficient to break off both pivots. In others, only one pivot suffers damage. One or both pivots bent is perhaps a more common fault caused by the endless jolting to which a modern wrist watch is subjected. To straighten a pivot considerable care is necessary. A quick look at the staff will tell you whether it is hard or only medium hard. All high-class watches have hardened and tempered parts, but the ordinary grade are content with a lesser degree of hardness.

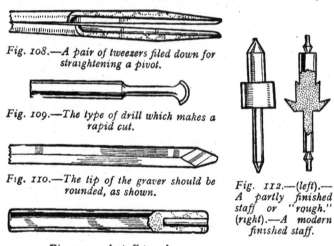

Fig. 108.—*A pair of tweezers filed down for straightening a pivot.*

Fig. 109.—*The type of drill which makes a rapid cut.*

Fig. 110.—*The tip of the graver should be rounded, as shown.*

Fig. 111.—*A staff punch.*

Fig. 112.—*(left).— A partly finished staff or "rough." (right).—A modern finished staff.*

A bent pivot can be straightened by placing a suitable sized watch bouchon (that is a short length of brass wire, drilled and turned at each end in the form of a bearing), over the bent pivot, and gently levering until the pivot is straight. To give control the bouchon should be held in a small pair of hand tongs. If the staff is very hard, it will be foolish to attempt to straighten a bent pivot without first reducing the hardness.

Remove the hairspring and roller, grasp the balance with an old pair of tweezers, and carefully warm the end of the staff over a small spirit flame until it turns blue. Another method is to heat a pair of pliers, and hold the end of the staff in the warmed pliers for a few seconds.

Straightening a Pivot.—An old pair of stout tweezers can be used effectively for straightening a pivot, if they are filed as shown in Fig. 108. When the pivot has been straightened, it will have to be re-polished, for it will have suffered through contact with the jewel hole and endstone. If there are any burrs the pivot file should be used very lightly for a few strokes will soon reduce both length and diameter of the pivot to its detriment. The polisher should be used with long steady strokes, whilst the staff is revolved at an even speed in the lathe. Charge the polisher first with oilstone dust, and finally with diamantine.

Although pivoting—the repairing of a broken staff by drilling and inserting a new pivot—was not tolerated by the old school of watchmakers, it is a popular method of repair when one pivot is badly damaged or broken. It is comparatively easy to pivot the upper half of a balance staff, as this is quite large. In fact, a hole can be drilled in the hairspring shoulder, and a fairly large plug fitted. More care is needed when drilling the lower half, which carries the roller, as this is always of smaller diameter. To pivot a staff, first stone off the broken end with an Arkansas slip and place the staff in a suitable lathe chuck.

Drilling Operation.—With a well-sharpened, long-pointed graver, catch the centre, and make a small sink in the end for a starting point for the drill. It is imperative that there should be no pip in the centre of sink. If there is, the hole will be out of true. Either select or make a drill a little larger than the finished pivot is to be, preferably a short drill with plenty of clearance, for it is surprising how quickly these tiny drills break if there is the slightest binding in the hole. If the staff is hard, the drill will have to be left hard, too, but as hard drills are liable to break off in the hole, it is better to reduce the hardness as described in a previous paragraph, and use a tempered drill.

If the drill fails to cut, do not continue the pressure or the surface will become burnished, and impossible to cut. It may be that the drill is not quite hard enough or the cutting edge may be too flat or too blunt. A little experiment with the

Arkansas slip will soon give good results. Fig. 109 shows the type of drill which gives a good cut when used with steel. The lathe drill differs only from the bow drill in that it needs only one cutting edge. When drilling, remove the drill periodically, insert a sharpened piece of pegwood, and gently revolve the staff. This will clean out the hole, as well as showing the depth of the hole on the pegwood.

Fitting a Pivot.—The hole should be as deep as the length of the intended pivot. File to a very slight taper a piece of hardened and tempered steel wire, small enough to just enter the hole. Then draw file it (draw filing consists of drawing the file up and down instead of the backward and forward movement), until it enters about two-thirds of the hole. Stone off

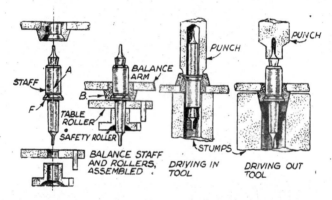

Fig. 113.—*The Waltham taper shoulder detachable staff. It is not riveted. The use of tapers enables the old staff to be knocked out and the new inserted without risk of distorting the balance.*

the end, dip it into some dry oilstone dust and push into the hole. Cut the pivot almost to length, stone the end, place the staff on a suitable stake, and complete the operation by driving the pivot home with a few light taps.

Replace the staff in the lathe, and turn the new pivot to the correct shape and size. It will be a good plan to round off the tip of the graver as shown in Fig. 110. This will make turning the conical part of the pivot less difficult. The pivot proper must be parallel and should be turned down until it just enters the jewel hole. Polishing should reduce the size of the pivot so that it is free without sideshake. The pivot should be polished on the jacot drum. The jacot drum is a round steel block fitting in the tailstock of the lathe, and furnished with a number of grooves each of which can be centred.

The Polisher.—The polisher can be made from a piece of soft steel, the edge of which should be filed to fit the conical part of the pivot. Use oilstone dust first, then diamantine. Be certain that the polisher and the groove in the jacot drum are clean before changing the polishing medium. Finish with a hard steel burnisher. Some watchmakers prefer to round the end of the pivot, others to leave it flat. When burnishing the end, the burnisher should be used from the pivot over the end. Burrs may be raised if the burnisher is used in the opposite direction.

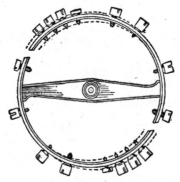

Fig. 114.—The principle of the compensating balance. The hairspring expands under heat, thus making the watch lose. The balance being bi-metallic, becomes smaller and thus is self-compensating. The reverse action takes place when temperature drops.

Fitting a new balance staff to a watch to-day is a fairly simple procedure, for so many watches have standardised parts that it is only necessary to quote the name, size and type of watch to receive a new staff that will need practically no adjustment. Occasionally, one does find it necessary to make a small adjustment. The staff may be a little too long, or the lower half of the staff may be a little too large to receive the roller. A little attention with the lathe and a graver will soon rectify matters. A little trouble may be experienced with the shoulder upon which the balance is riveted. I have often found the shoulder a little too small. This unfortunate condition can be improved by using a round-faced shallow punch that just fits over the staff. Rotate punch, balance and staff at the same time as the riveting blows are delivered. When the balance is firm the staff can be given a few sharp taps to swell the head of the rivet. Fig. 111 shows the type of punch.

The Staffs.—Interchangeable staffs are not available for all watches, especially some of the older, but nevertheless reliable, movements. This fact makes the turning of a new staff still an important section of watch repairing. The first step is to examine the old staff in its position in the movement, and notice the clearance of the balance between the centre wheel and the pallet bridge. Remove the top and bottom endpieces, replace the balance bridge and take the overall length from jewel hole to jewel hole with a measuring gauge. (Watchmakers use a douzième gauge divided into twelfths of a ligne.)

Turning the First Section.—Place the balance and staff in a suitable lathe chuck and with a long-pointed and well-sharpened graver turn away the rivet that secures the balance to the staff. Do not turn away any of the balance arms, or the timekeeping will be disturbed. When the rivet has been turned away, place the balance and staff on a block having different sized holes. Choose a hole that will just take the balance shoulder to prevent any distortion of the balance. Rest a small hollow punch on the hairspring shoulder, and drive out the staff with a sharp blow. Select a partly finished staff or "rough" that is a little larger than the old staff. Fig. 112 shows a "rough."

The first section to be turned is the largest from which is shaped the back slope and balance shoulder. Turn the back slope and polish it. Change the chuck, reverse the staff and turn the lower part of the staff to receive the roller. An approximate idea of the size can be made by measurement, but the roller should be tried before final polishing. A clean-cut effect will be produced by cutting into the already polished portion. Reverse the staff again and cut into the back slope for the balance shoulder, try the balance until it just enters. The actual seat should be undercut slightly in order that the balance sits flat. The top part of the balance shoulder should be well undercut to form a good rivet. The hairspring shoulder is next turned and the back slope for the top pivot and both polished, and the pivot turned until it just enters the jewel hole. Reverse the staff, turn the back slope for the bottom pivot and polish it, and turn the bottom pivot.

Measure the staff and turn off any superfluous metal. **Fig. 112** shows a modern finished staff.

Polishing and Burnishing.—The pivots should next be polished and burnished as previously described. Drive the balance on the staff, but do not rivet. Place the balance and staff in the movement, and examine the truth of the balance. The freedom of the pivots can also be tested. Replace the endpieces and turn the movement from one side to the other, and listen for the drop of the staff from endstone to endstone. If the staff is free a metallic note will be distinctly heard. Remove the balance and staff and rivet the balance to the staff. A good fitting balance should need little riveting.

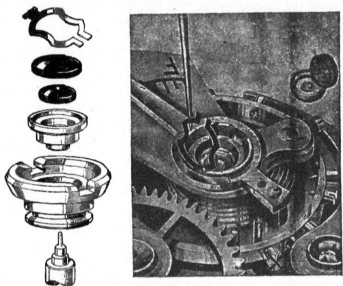

Fig. 114a.—*The Incabloc shock-absorber which is fitted to the balance staff jewel holes. It also enables the end stone to be removed for oiling the pivots without removing the balance cock.*

Neither should there be any need to skim the rivet in the lathe. If the balance has been put out of truth by riveting it should be corrected in the usual way with brass-nosed pliers. A pair of jewelled calipers with an adjustable truing slide will be more convenient than the movement for testing. When the balance is true drive on the roller, replace the hairspring and the staff is completed.

CHAPTER XII

ADJUSTING THE BALANCE AND OTHER PARTS

THE balance, before being removed, should be thoroughly examined as it is one of the, if not the most, important parts of the watch. If the balance is not vibrating lead it around sufficiently with the tweezers-point to cause it to vibrate, and watch the action. The balance wheel should have no "up-and-down" movement as it revolves, and when viewed from above the wheel should be perfectly circular. Any irregularity in this direction will have an adverse effect on the time-keeping. The type of balance likely to give most trouble in this way is the bi-metallic compensation type—a balance consisting of two metals fused together, usually brass and steel and having the rim cut right through in two places to allow for expansion and contraction as ex-

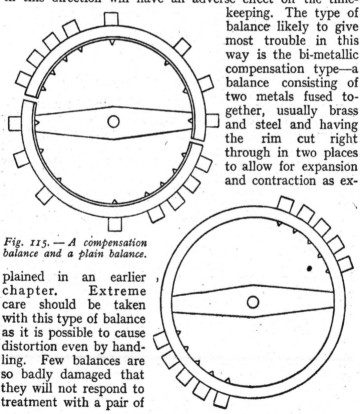

Fig. 115. — A compensation balance and a plain balance.

plained in an earlier chapter. Extreme care should be taken with this type of balance as it is possible to cause distortion even by handling. Few balances are so badly damaged that they will not respond to treatment with a pair of tweezers or brass-nosed pliers, but there is really no cure for a balance which is very much "out-of-round." A new balance is the only remedy. Fig. 115 shows a plain balance and a compensation balance.

Curb Pins.—Examine also the clearance between the arms of the balance wheel and the bottom of the hairspring stud—the small detachable block to which the end of the hairspring is pinned—and the curb pins—the two pins in the regulator. Little trouble is likely with curb pins which are of the two-pin type, but the type which consists of one pin and a movable block often called the boot piece or the buckle needs more careful attention. Fig. 116 shows the two types of curb pins. The sole of the boot piece is often left too thick, thereby

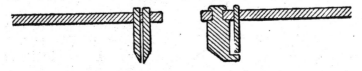

Fig. 116.—Two types of curb pins.

leaving only very little clearance between it and the arms of the balance. As the object of the boot piece is to prevent other coils of the hairspring from being caught in the curb pins there is no necessity for the sole to be left thick. It is quite a simple matter to reduce the thickness with a fine file when the regulator has been removed from the balance bridge. Lay the regulator upside-down on a boxwood block and turn the boot piece to the closed position. Hold the regulator down with the forefinger, and with the second finger as a guide to the safety edge of the file make one or two forward cuts until the thickness has been reduced to a minimum. Re-cut the screwdriver slot with a slitting file if it appears to be shallow. Before replacing the regulator it is advisable to file off the outside corner of the boot piece. This will prevent the points of extra long balance screws from fouling it when the watch is lying in a dial-up position.

Endshake.—The small amount of free space between the ends of the pivot and the flat surface of the end-stones is known as endshake—in the case of ordinary train wheels between the shoulder of the pivot and the jewel hole—and correct endshake is an important condition in any watch.

Too much endshake is as great an evil as no endshake.

Very little of the jewel hole is actual bearing surface. Should, therefore, there be too much endshake, there will be a tendency for one or other of the pivots to come out of the bearing hole, when the watch is in either a "dial up" or "dial down" position. When one pivot is resting on an endstone the other pivot of the balance would have every opportunity of fouling the curb pins, the hairspring stud, centre wheel, and pallet bridge. Contact with any of these would spell disaster. Fig. 117 shows a pivot in a jewel hole with the correct amount of endshake. When one pivot is resting on an endshake the other pivot should be just clear of the other endstone. In some cases it is possible to tell whether a balance had endshake by turning the movement first one way and then the other way and listening to the drop of the balance; the sound will be decidedly metallic. With brass set jewels excessive endshake can be corrected by reducing the shoulder of the brass jewel setting. Whichever setting is altered will depend to a certain extent upon the position of the roller with the pallet fork.

Adjusting the Jewels.—If the upper disc of the roller is so near the fork as to be likely to cause friction in certain positions, the bottom jewel must be raised. If the roller adjustments are correct the top jewel should be lowered. It is quite possible the jewel screws will not keep the endpiece tight after such an alteration. The quickest and neatest way to overcome this trouble is to select a new brass set endstone, place it in a suitable lathe chuck, and turn it to fit, leaving it flush with the plate. Insufficient importance is given to jewel settings, for one frequently finds watches with loose balance and other jewels. It is quite easy to appreciate the amount of friction created when a pivot is rotating in a jewel hole and the jewel hole itself is moving in its setting.

There should be a reasonable amount of clearance between the underside of the balance wheel and the upper surface of the pallet bridge. As long as daylight can be seen between these two surfaces, it will signify that they do not touch, but with such a small margin, the smallest speck of dirt or tiniest hair is quite likely to impede the vibration of the balance.

The Pallet Bridge.—To be on the safe side it is advisable to reduce the thickness of the pallet bridge. Remove the bridge and place it upon a piece of cork, and with a sharp file carefully reduce the surface. Exercise great care, for it is easy to bend a delicate bridge of this type. Brush away any file dust and try the clearance. Some balances carry a number

of timing washers—very small washers placed under some of
the balance screws to bring the watch to time—and occasionally a washer hangs below the rim of the balance, an unsus-
pecting evil.   Do not attempt to file away the washer.   Reduce
the thickness of the pallet bridge if there is still insufficient
clearance.

The clearance between the pallets and the underside of the
pallet bridge should also be closely examined.   With most

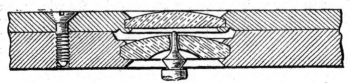

Fig 117.—*A pivot in a jewel hole with the correct amount of
endshake*

Fig. 118.—*A section of the pallets and pallet bridge.*

modern watches the upper pallet pivot should rise so short
that there is hardly any clearance, and I have often seen
bright marks on the pallet arms made by contact with the
pallet bridge.   This contact is caused by the jewel hole being
set too high.   To prevent this friction file off the corner of the
bridge from the underside and reduce the general thickness.
File carefully, for should the jewel setting be disturbed, the
bridge will be ruined.   Fig. 118 shows a section of the pallets
and pallet bridge.

CHAPTER XIII

CORRECTING A BALANCE AND REPAIRING HAIRSPRINGS

THE balance and hairspring are handled by some repairers with the minimum rather than the maximum of care, but they should always be treated with respect, for the timekeeping properties of a watch are governed by the action of these two important parts. No attempt can be made with regulation unless the balance is in perfect poise. This means that the balance should have no heavy point, but remain stationary when placed in any position. Faults in timekeeping are often traced to the variation of the balance vibrations when the watch is in different positions. "Positional errors" as they are called are due to a balance with an uneven distribution of weight.

Correcting a Balance.—To correct such a balance the usual method is to employ a poising tool as shown in Fig. 119, which consists of two adjustable knife edges. The hairspring is removed, but the roller is left in its correct position. The knife edges are operated by means of the adjusting screw until each pivot rests on a knife edge. A slight turning will be sufficient to discover the heavy point if the balance is out of poise. Several methods can be used for removing excess weight. One or more sinks can be made in the underside of the balance rim (at the lowest point) with a small chamfering tool.

Another method is to reduce the head of a screw with a file and re-polish it—be sure never to touch either of the four quarters timing screws. An easier method, and one which can be applied to high-class balances, is to make the slit in the offending screw a little deeper with a screw-head file. In this way the weight will be reduced, but the balance will not be defaced. Of course, it may be necessary to treat several screws before the balance is equi-poised. When a watch is in a horizontal position an out-of-poise balance has no effect, but should the watch be placed in a hanging position, a gain or loss will be noticeable according to the position of the error. Some inferior watches which are tested in only two positions —"dial up" and pendant down (in the case of wrist watches) —have their balances actually left out of poise to counteract the going slow in the pendant down position—an effective but somewhat crude form of compensation.

Over Compensated Watches.—Occasionally, a watch is found to be over-compensated, which means that it goes fast in hot weather. To correct this, weight must be removed from the free ends of the balance rim towards the balance arms. This is done by taking a screw from each of the free ends of the rim, and screwing it in a hole nearer the arms. An insufficiently compensated watch is one which goes slow in hot weather, and to overcome this difficulty all the weight must be concentrated at the free ends of the rim by removing one or more screws to the extreme ends of the rim.

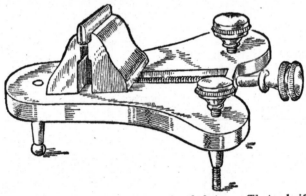

Fig. 119.—A poising tool for correcting the balance. The two knife edges are adjusted to clear the balance, and the stand must be perfectly horizontal. When poised, the balance will remain stationary in any position. A heavy spot will swing to the lowest point.

The original flat type of hairspring has been succeeded by the Breguet or over-coil hairspring for precision timekeeping, and the majority of good-class watches are now so fitted. The considerable expansion and contraction of the coils of a flat hairspring are continually moving the centre of gravity from one side to the other. This movement of the centre of gravity has the same effect upon timekeeping as a balance out-of-poise. In a Breguet hairspring the last coil is bent upwards, and across the other coils to the hairspring stud. The shape of the over-coil follows a definite theoretical curve (the Breguet curve) and is of such a shape that during the expansion and contraction of the coils the position of the centre of gravity remains unaltered. Fig. 120 shows a typical overcoil curve.

A Damaged Spring.—Should it be necessary to replace a damaged Breguet spring two methods can be adopted. The first method consists of making alterations in the curve until the spring has a perfectly concentric movement—a method which takes time, and not one to be recommended, for a spring which has had considerable bending is of little use. The second method, which is easier and better, is to obtain a series of pattern drawings, and lay the spring on the particular drawing and bend until it corresponds in size, and shape to the curve as depicted.

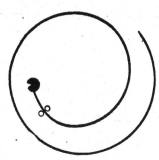

Fig. 120.—*A typical Overcoil curve (The Phillip).*

Fig. 121.—*Re-colleting a damaged hairspring.*

Select a new spring that is approximately half the diameter of the balance and pin it to the collet. Break away sufficient of the centre of the spring to free the collet, and bend the end of the spring inwards almost at right-angles, make the end straight and a little longer than the hole in the collet. File a long pin to fit the collet hole, and file a flat upon it. Place a small piece of the spring in the hole and push in the pin. Make a mark on the pin at each end of the hole as shown in Fig. 121. Withdraw the pin, cut off the small end, partly sever the other end, and remove any burrs. Place the collet upon a broach of similar tapered tool, place the spring in the hole, push in the pin—not too tight—and break it off. Be certain that the spring is perfectly flat before pushing the pin tight, for any movement here will have a disastrous effect upon timekeeping.

The spring should not be finally fixed to the collet until the position of attachment of the inner coil has been determined. The spring usually comes away from the collet at one of four points on a cross whose centre is the centre of the collet, and whose arms are parallel to two lines drawn at right-angles to each other through the centre of the movement as in Fig. 122. The various positions have a gaining, losing, or negative effect upon the rate of the watch. A table showing the different effects should be consulted in conjunction with the particular type of watch under repair. In a watch in which the "pendant-up" position is the most used the spring usually comes away at right-angles to a line drawn parallel to the "pendant-up" position. In the case of precis on watches the inner curve, too, is theoretically designed; in any case the spring should have no angular bends, for such bends are against the natural form of the spring.

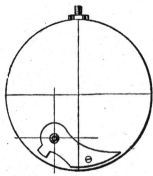

Fig. 122.—In a watch used mostly in the pendant up position the spring "comes away" at right-angles to a line drawn parallel to the pendant vertical.

Fig. 123.—Using two pairs of tweezers to adjust the coil of the spring. The type of tweezers to use for bending the overcoil is shown on page 31. Use of these avoids kinks.

The Count.—The hairspring (now colleted), should be placed upon the balance staff in order to ascertain the "count." The "count" refers to the number of vibrations the balance will make in an hour. Although there are rates above and below, the majority of watches (both pocket and wrist) have balances which vibrate 18,000 times an hour. The most satisfactory way of counting the new spring is to use one of the many balance counting tools, a special piece of apparatus often supplied with three standard balances of different rates. The balance being tested is held above the standard balance, and the two vibrated together until each has the same rate.

A new spring can be counted with the aid of a pocket chronograph or stop watch. Hold the outer coil with a pair of tweezers, and let the broken balance pivot rest on the glass of the stop watch. Start the balance vibrating before the seconds hand reaches the zero mark. An 18,000 balance will give 150 alternate vibrations in 1 minute. If the balance vibrates slower grasp more of the outer coil, and vice-versa; when

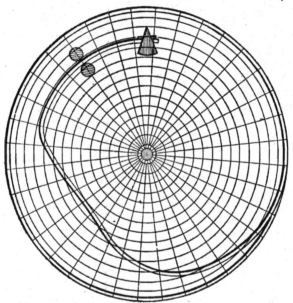

Fig. 124.—*Template for forming Breguet curve or overcoil. Special hollow-point tweezers are available for bending the overcoil, upon the correct shape of which isochronism and the elimination of position errors depend.*

the balance is vibrating correctly make a scratch on the spring. As this point represents the part that will be between the regulator pins, leave sufficient spring to reach the stud and break off any waste.

Overcoil.—No hard-and-fast rule can be laid down with regard to the upward bend. Some favour a gradual bend, others a sharp bracket bend. Each springer has his own favourite idea and special tools are made for the purpose. A pattern should be selected which corresponds as nearly as possible to the diameter of the spring, and which has the same measurement from centre to stud as the distance between the jewel hole and hairspring stud on the balance bridge. Remove the spring from the balance and lay it upon the corresponding pattern. The "count" mark is placed upon the line drawn on the pattern. The outer coil is gripped at about three-quarters of a turn from the end with a stout pair of tweezers, and pulled upwards with another pair of tweezers. The curve is next formed according to the pattern. That part of the spring from the "count" mark to the end will be concentric. Using the two pairs of tweezers hold the spring at the end of the incline and lever up the terminal curve until it is parallel with the other coils of the spring as shown in Fig. 123. The shape of the curve is also governed by the distance the regulator pins are from the centre of the jewel hole. When the pins are almost in a line with the circumference of the spring, the curve will have a straight section. This straight section is reduced to an even curve the nearer the pins come to the centre. The completed hairspring should now be replaced on the balance, the balance put in the watch and the cock screwed down. The "count" mark should be placed between the regulator pins; the end of the spring, if the curve has been made properly, should now be in line with the pin-hole in the stud, and should only need the slightest touch to put it in the hole. Make a small pin in the same way as described for pinning the spring to the collet, and secure the spring to the stud, not tight, however, until the regulator moves freely without altering the shape of the spring.

Temperature Tests.—Temperature tests are made in an icebox at about 30°F. and in an oven at about 90°F. and last for 24 hours; any adjustment is made by moving the temperature screws to or from the free ends of the balance rim, as previously described. A test in the middle temperature is advisable to restore the balance to its original position. There are a number of positional tests, the usual being pendant up, pendant down, pendant right, pendant left, dial up and dial down. The time of the vibration should be the same both in the long and short arcs. In other words, it should be isochronous. The vertical positions lessen the arc of vibration. If there are no errors due to faulty escapement, pallets out-of-poise, bad jewel holes, or ruby pin too tight in the fork, the quarter screws can be screwed in or out as required.

CHAPTER XIV

FITTING TEETH, JEWELS AND HANDS

FREQUENTLY when a mainspring breaks, the shock is sufficient to bend or even break a tooth in the barrel or centre wheel. A new tooth can be fitted in the following manner. First gauge the thickness of the barrel, then drill a hole at the base of the broken tooth. The drill should be a little smaller than an existing tooth, and the hole should be a little deeper than a tooth. The depth of the hole can be tested with a piece of pegwood.

When repairing a large barrel, file up a piece of steel wire until it partly enters the hole, draw file it and drive it home, carefully, to avoid bulging the barrel face. If there is any doubt about the grip of the new tooth, fuse a minute piece of solder about the tooth before dressing it to the shape of the existing teeth with a needle file. A piece of brass wire will be strong enough for a small-size barrel. The barrel and the centre wheel should be put between the plates to test the gearing before re-assembling the movement.

Fitting teeth to either the centre, third or fourth wheels is an even more delicate operation. The holes should be drilled right through the rim. A piece of brass wire held in a pin vice or pin tong and filed to a very gradual taper should be forced in. Any surplus wire should be cut off and the new tooth filed to shape. If necessary a little solder can be applied to the inside of the rim. Should the wheel be too thin to drill, a new tooth can be fitted in another way. Select a broken wheel of similar size, cut out a block of about three teeth, and break off the end teeth. Clean the rim of the wheel and the new tooth in readiness for soldering. Lay the new tooth upon the rim of the wheel and solder it in the correct position.

When fixed the new tooth should be filed to the exact shape and finally faced off with a polishing buff. The tooth should be fixed to that side of the centre wheel which has most clearance. A new tooth can be fitted to a cylinder escape wheel by a similar method if the cylinder has a fairly large opening. Procure an old escape wheel of the same size and break off one tooth from the rim. The new tooth is then laid in position and soldered to the escape wheel rim. Place the wheel on a small brass plate or blueping pan which has been previously warmed. It is essential that the heel of the new tooth does not project beyond the diameter of the wheel teeth. (See Figs. 126 to 128.)

The brass set jewel hole and the jewel hole retained by a burnished flange were both described in another chapter. Modern watches, however, use a different method of jewel retention. The jewel holes have perfectly straight sides. Early type jewels needed only an opening and closing tool, but to fit the latest type a small press as supplied with a jewel outfit is necessary to ensure correct fit.

Small glass bottles similar to those used for ordinary jewel holes contain the graduated plug-type jewels—often called friction jewels—whose size ranges from 0·70 mm. to 3·00 mm., each size varying by 1/100 mm. The press has a stop divided into 1/100 mm. which regulates the depth to which the plunger may be depressed. A number of fittings include stakes, pushers, clampers and broaches. The broaches are actually tapered half-round cutters; unlike an ordinary broach the taper end is of perfectly circular formation in order that the sides of the finished hole may be straight.

As the amount of endshake varies the face of a jewel hole may be above or below the surface of the watch plate. Before pushing out the old jewel measure the position on the press. This is done by depressing the pusher until it touches the jewel and then adjusting the finely divided stop. A reading should be taken to ensure a correct fit with the new jewel. The old jewel should be pushed out from the outside. First select a broach which will only slightly enlarge the existing hole. The hole is broached from the inside with a gentle turning action, a little pressure being applied until the cylindrical part of the broach passes through the plate.

After broaching, slightly chamfer the edge to remove any burrs. The chamfered edge will also act as a guide for the jewel hole which has one edge bevelled. Choose a jewel with a suitable hole and which is 1/100 mm. larger than the broach—a broach which measures 1·99 mm. will need a jewel which measures 2·00 mm. If the face of the jewel is to be flush with the plate, use a pusher larger than the jewel. Lay the jewel in position on the watch plate which should be resting on one of the solid stakes, and depress the plunger until it touches the plate. The previously recorded setting should be used for jewels which have to be above or below the surface.

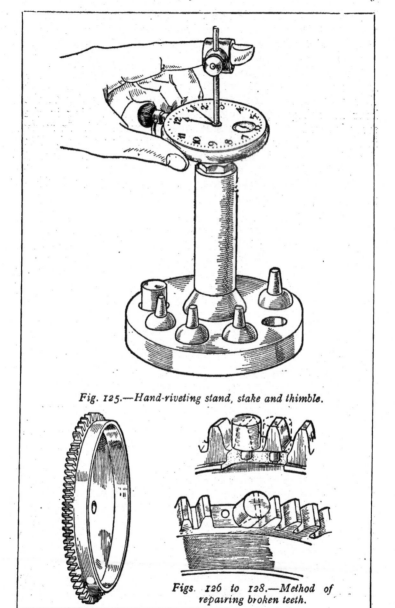

Fig. 125.—Hand-riveting stand, stake and thimble.

Figs. 126 to 128.—Method of repairing broken teeth.

This type of jewelling need not be confined to modern watches as the old-fashioned burnished in settings can be broached out to receive a larger jewel hole. Brass set jewels and bushes can be efficiently fitted with this press.

Watch hands are too often regarded as an odd pair of fingers which point to the time. They should, however, be chosen and fitted with care. Many stoppages are due to the hour hand being too long, its point either catching in the seconds hand or the under side of the minute hand. In many instances the hour hand is as long as the minute hand. The size of the socket is most important, and to obtain a correct fit certain gauges are essential. One gauge for reading the size of the hour wheel socket or cannon pinion resembles a pivot or mainspring gauge.

Fig. 128a.—A useful press for jewels, staffs, pinions, etc.

Graduated-in in 1/10 mm., two gauges are necessary to cover the whole range. The smaller of the two records from 25/100 mm. to 100/100 mm., whilst the larger reads from 100/100 mm. to 200/100 mm. Frequently the sockets of broken hands are still in position. When these are available a different kind of gauge can be used which consists of three tapered steel needles. The socket is pushed over the needle where its size is indicated on the scale. These needle gauges also have a scale which indicates the length of hand required. Cards of broachless hands are obtainable for use with these gauges. As the name implies fitting can be carried out without the use of broaches.

Minute and seconds hands must, however, be broached out to fit the cannon pinion and seconds pivot respectively. Hand holders are available.

CHAPTER XV

WATCH CASE REPAIRS

THE watch case is too often treated as an ornamental box which holds the movement rather than an important part of the whole assembly. Many watches suffer from the fault of being fitted into inferior cases—the type often offered for sale as *solid* gold cases—solid, of course, but the total weight barely ever exceeds two penny weights The watch case should always be strong enough to protect the movement from damage as well as exclude the dust.

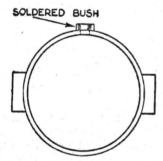

SOLDERED BUSH

Fig. 129.—Bushing a worn winder hole.

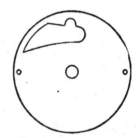

Fig. 130. — Method of relieving a "close" case.

Case troubles present many difficulties; probably the most common source whereby dust and dirt enter the movement is through a worn winder hole or pendant as it is called. To cure this fault, take a piece of brass bush wire a little larger than the hole, place it in a suitable lathe chuck and turn it down until it just fits the hole in the case. Cut it off; leaving a small shoulder as shown in Fig. 129. The bush must not protrude too far into the case to interfere with the movement. To secure the bush apply a little flux and a very small piece of solder to the inside of the case and gently warm over a small gas or spirit flame. When soldered open the hole with a broach until the winding shaft is just free to turn.

Some gold cases have a very thin back, so thin in fact, that the back end of the centre pinion and other raised parts of the movement make an impression on the back when the watch is worn, a very undesirable state of affairs as the pressure is likely to create friction with a consequent erratic rate. Considerable improvement can be made by soldering an old hour hand to the back of the case over the indent caused by the centre pinion. The socket will now rest upon the back plate and keep the back of the case away from the movement.

A very difficult "case" in which the balance staff was damaged by the case being gripped tight was cured by making

Fig. 131.—A joint pusher which consists of a slender steel punch fitted with a handle.

STOPPING

Fig. 132.—Details of the joint pin.

a brass disc to fit inside the case back. As well as a hole being drilled to free the centre pinion, a hole resembling the balance bridge was cut in the disk with a piercing saw thereby removing undue pressure from the balance staff. Two small holes were drilled at the edge of the disc by which the disc was soldered to the back of the case. Fig. 130 gives an idea of the disc.

Many a watch has sustained damage through a worn or broken loop; to-day however there is less risk as the strap attachment is very often a sturdy built-in affair. When a wire loop is broken away from the case at one side or even both sides it is a fairly simple matter to refix it. With some cases holes are drilled in the band of the case and the loops inserted before being hard-soldered, with others the loops are only fixed on to the surface. If holes are drilled to receive the loop it will be easier to adjust it into position before securing it with a piece of soft iron binding wire.

Black iron binding wire is used to minimise the risk of its being fused to the article being soldered. Before "rigging" up a case for brazing both the back and the bezel should be removed. To do this drive out the joint pins or hinge pins as they are sometimes called. These pins are usually inserted from the right-hand side when holding the back or bezel towards the body. Apart from the ill effect of the intense heat upon the joints or hinges the removal of the back and bezel will prevent unnecessary polishing.

When the loop has been bound into position everything is ready for fixing Brazing, hard soldering or gold and silver soldering is rather different from soft soldering. A different solder and a different flux have to be used, also an intense heat is necessary to fuse the metals. To prepare the flux take a crystal of borax and rub it down on a piece of wet slate until it produces a creamy paste.

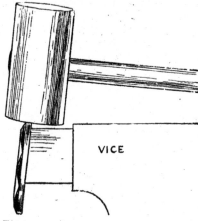

Fig. 133.—Contracting a bezel in a vice.

Sharpen a piece of plywood to a chisel shape and apply a little borax paste to the parts to be brazed. A small piece of solder should be placed into position and the case put on a piece of charcoal or asbestos.

First, gently warm the case all over, for a sudden application of heat to the borax and solder will cause the borax to bubble up and deposit solder anywhere except in the desired spot. As soon as the solder has settled the heat can be directed on to the parts which are to be brazed. For small and lightweight cases an ordinary mouth blow-pipe will be suitable as the heat can be more easily controlled. Immediately the solder glistens stop blowing as this will be the signal that the metals have fused.

As soon as the case is cold the binding wire can be removed. The case, especially around the loop will be badly discoloured; the discoloured parts will have to be treated before the case can be re-polished. Any surplus borax will have assumed a glazed and brittle state, but this can be removed with a few light blows from a small watchmaker's hammer. A gold case can be cleaned with some strong hydrochloric acid applied with a sharpened piece of wood.

Hydrochloric acid will leave the case a pale green colour, the case, however, can soon be restored to its original gold colour with the aid of a little machine buffing and a final application of rouge. A slightly different method of cleaning has to be adopted after brazing a silver case. When the surplus borax has been removed the case is re-heated (not a red heat) and immersed in some "pickle" (slightly diluted sulphuric acid).

Allow the case to remain in the "pickle" for five or ten minutes. When removed from the "pickle", the case which will be a creamy colour, should be well rinsed in water, preferably warm. By scratch brushing the case with stale beer a brand new finish can be produced, plus a course of final buffing with rouge. (A scratch brush is a brush having bristles of fine brass wire.) The small brass wire bristles sold for cleaning suede shoes are quite suitable for this work. Stubborn stains can be easily removed by rubbing the affected part with a little powdered pumice.

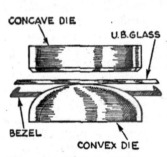

Fig. 134.—*Method of fitting unbreakable crystal.*

The replacement of a complete hinge (back or front) is not a common repair, the replacement of the centre portion is, however, frequently necessary. The first step is to remove the joint pin or hinge pin as it is sometimes called. Usually the pin is inserted from right to left; but as it may be inserted from left to right care must be exercised in driving out the pin. Too much pressure in the wrong direction will easily split the hinge or joint (charnière) as it is usually called.

In some instances a push with a joint pusher (a slender steel punch fitted with a handle—see Fig. 131) will be sufficient to remove the pin, in others a few taps with a small hammer may be necessary. High grade cases usually have a short joint pin which is inserted well within the three joint sections, the open ends being filled with a "stopping" of gold or silver. Before the joint pin can be taken out these "stoppings" have to be removed. A well-sharpened graver will be the most effective tool to remove these "stoppings" which are entered from each end. Fig. 132 shows this type of joint.

When the back, the bezel, and broken joint have been removed, preparations can be made to affix a new joint. A very shallow groove should be filed with a round file at the original joint position. Select a suitable sized piece of gold or silver charnière and cut off sufficient to make a new joint; the joint should be filed until it just fits the joints on the back. Next, the charnière is laid with its seam downwards in the groove on the band of the case and tied with soft iron binding wire. Borax should be made and applied as described when brazi..g a loop and a narrow piece of solder slipped between the binding wire to enable it to flow around the base and seam of the charnière. After soldering the case should be cleaned and polished as previously described. It is better to use too little rather than too much solder as any excess will be difficult to remove.

Before filing up a new brass joint pin the three joints should be broached out to prevent binding. The centre joint should be a trifle larger than

Fig. 135.—*How the cork chucks are made.*

the others, as it is bad practice to see the joint pin turning with the back and bezel. When the pin has been filed to fit it should be cut off to the required length about $\frac{1}{16}$ inch shorter each end than the length of the joint. After the joint pin has been inserted the "stoppings" (gold or silver) should be fitted.

The loss of a bezel is a frequent occurrence with the strap-on and two-piece case. A loose bezel needs to be contracted or the case expanded. To contract the bezel, first remove the glass then place the bezel on a circular stake or hammer-head, which has been fixed in a vice as shown in Fig. 133, and gently tap the edge all around with a light mallet. Pliers should never be used as these only kink the edge. A hinged bezel which has been strained can be made to snap if a needle is placed between the bezel and the band of the case near the hinge and the bezel forced downwards.

The most popular watch glass is the unbreakable, more correctly called the unbreakable watch crystal. These crystals can be obtained in a complete range of sizes both round and fancy shaped, gauged in millimetres. To fit a crystal, first make sure that the bezel groove is clean cut, next measure the diameter with a millimetre rule. Unlike ordinary watch glasses these crystals are flat and the necessary curvature is produced by fitting an oversize crystal.

The curvature for most watches can be produced by selecting a crystal 2 millimetres larger. The press used for fitting these crystals is a simple affair consisting of a number of wooden dies, concave and convex. The bezel is placed over the lower or convex and the crystal placed on the die, the upper or concave die is then pressed on to the crystal until it is domed sufficiently to enter the bezel. If the bezel is an in-between size it may be necessary to cut out a crystal specially. Take a square of unbreakable material, place the bezel on the square and mark around it, next cut out the circle with a pair of scissors.

The cork chucks used to turn the crystal are quite simple to construct. Procure two pieces of steel both about $\frac{3}{4}$ in. long, which will fit No. 50 chuck; on the end of one turn a shoulder about $\frac{1}{8}$ in., on the other piece turn a shoulder at one end and a conical pivot at the other. A disc of brass should next be soldered to the shouldered end of each piece of steel as in Fig. 135. Two slices from a good cork can now be fixed to the discs with shellac or sealing wax and the cork chucks are finished.

The plain chuck is placed in No. 50 lathe chuck and the conical chuck in the female centre of the tail-stock. Place the unbreakable material between the corks and screw up the tail-stock. When true proceed to turn a bevelled edge with a well-sharpened graver. The rest should be well above the centre as the slightest dig will lift the crystal out of the corks. An "inside and outside" measuring rule is the best means of checking the size as this can be done without removing the crystal from the corks. When the crystal is 2 millimetres larger than the bezel it can be fitted in the usual way.

CHAPTER XVI

PRACTICAL HINTS

MAKE it a rule to test every watch you handle for magnetism. A small pocket compass placed close to the balance when the watch is running will indicate by a vibrating motion if the balance is polarised, and, if it is, the watch and case should be treated in a de-magnetiser, to remove this trouble.

When repairing a watch inspect the balance pivots carefully to see that they are straight and in good condition. Examine the endstones, and if they show any wear it should be polished off, by using a small lap made of tortoise-shell about 30 mm. in diameter, mounted in the lathe, and a small amount of fine diamond powder mixed with oil put on the face of it. By holding the pitted endstone against this with a slight pressure, while the lap is running at a fairly high speed, it can be made as good as a new one in a very short time.

After this operation it is important to clean the endstone and setting thoroughly.

Examine the balance to see that it is true and in poise.

Do not open the bankings carelessly. Remember that the result of excessive slide is a dead loss of power, and this loss increases rapidly with any deterioration of the oil on the pallet stones.

Do not neglect to try the jewel pin to see if it is set firmly. Even a slightly loose jewel pin is a fruitful source of trouble.

Do not open the curb pins on the regulator. The hairspring should fit between the pins, without pinching, and without play, to get the best result in timing.

See that the hairspring is centred and flat, and has a sufficient amount of clearance under all conditions. Bear in mind that its regular vibrations will be increased a good deal at times, when the watch is subjected to sudden motions or shocks.

Do not neglect to remove any finger-mark or greasy matter from the plates, caused by the handling of the movement. For this purpose I find a buff stick very useful—a flat stick of wood, about 14 mm. wide, covered on one side with buckskin, such as is used for buffing. The end of this is dipped in benzine, wiped off rapidly with a clean cloth, and used immediately for cleaning off the top surface of the plates.

Do not expect a position adjusted watch to rate the same as it did originally after any change or alteration has been made in the balance pivots, or balance jewels. Even when the work is done with the greatest care this kind of repair may call for readjusting the movement, and this should be done by a watchmaker experienced in this class of work.

Do not consider it a bad investment to put as much money as you can afford into up-to-date tools. And do not consider the time wasted which you spend in keeping your tools in good condition.

Do not neglect to keep abreast of the times by reading good books and papers pertaining to the trade.

I wish to emphasise to the young watchmaker the importance of practice or training in the various branches of his work; and would recommend, as a profitable way of spending some of his leisure time, to take, for example, a discarded balance, and bend it out of shape, and true and poise it repeatedly for the purpose of gaining experience. We might state that although a beginner may work on a balance all day, and still not succeed in getting it in very good order, an expert can do 20 to 25 in an hour, and get them all good. This applies equally well to the work on the hairspring, the escapement, the pivots, jewelling, and so on. And I would also state that nothing but hard work and conscientious application to the work, coupled with a certain amount of study, will ever bring forth a skilful and efficient workman.

How to Set a Jewel in a Watch Plate.—To replace a broken jewel which is set directly in the plate, first carefully remove all the pieces of the old jewel, mount the plate with the hole true in a pump centre jewelling head, or a universal head. Run the lathe slowly, and with a pointed burnisher carefully open the old bezel until the sides are parallel, and the diameter about the same as the original size. If the bezel is made any larger than the original size it is very likely to break. The usual way to put the new jewel in place is to wet the end of the finger and touch it to the jewel, which will adhere readily. Push it into the setting and slide the finger off. This will leave the bezel and jewel wet, and hold the jewel while the bezel is being closed over it.

The form of tool used for burnishing down the bezel is snown in Fig. 136. This tool is held firmly on the T-rest at the proper height, the bevelled side towards the hole, as shown in Fig. 136. With the lathe running slowly, it is forced towards the plate until the bezel is closed firmly over the edge of the jewel as in Fig. 135.

If the bezel is broken, a jewel of the same outside diameter as the original one may sometimes be set securely by making a new bezel of larger diameter and burnishing it in far enough to cover the edge of the jewel. This is done by starting the burnisher at a point farther way from the jewel, as shown in Fig. 136. If the metal around the hole is cut away to such an extent that this method is impracticable, it will be necessary to either select a jewel of larger outside diameter, or put a metal bushing in the plate large enough to make a new setting of the diameter required for the new jewel.

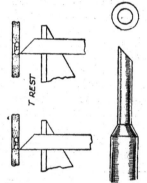

Fig. 136.—*Method of setting a jewel in a watch plate.*

To Remove a Broken Screw from a Watch Plate.—After all other screws and steelwork are removed suspend the plate on a copper wire in a saturated solution of alum in water. If the screw which is to be removed is very long it is necessary to take the plate from the solution every 24 hours, and with a sharp point remove the dissolved steel, in order to hasten the action of the solution.

Waltham Screw Taps.—The table on page 160 gives the pitch, the diameter of the thread and also the proper size of the tap drill, for all the screws used in the Waltham Watch movements. Taps of all these sizes are furnished by the Company at a nominal price.

To find which is the right tap for any of the screws used in Waltham watch movements, measure the diameter of the screw and refer to the table. If the screw measures ·65 for example, we find that ·65 in the column of diameters of threads corresponds to No. 17 tap, for which the tap drill should measure ·54.

The only threads which we are unable to identify by measuring their diameters are Nos. 7 and 13, but in this instance the difference in pitch is sufficient to show at a glance in comparing one with the other.

Mainspring Don'ts.—DON'T fail to provide yourself with the best mainspring winder that can be obtained. See that the hooks on all arbors of the winders are no longer than the thickness of the thinnest spring, and thus avoid kinking, and, therefore, unnecessary breaking of mainsprings.

DON'T use a mainspring that is too long, because it fills the barrel and prevents that part, or the mainwheel, from making the required number of revolutions, with the consequence that the watch will not run as long as it should after each winding.

DON'T use a mainspring that is too strong, because it will set, increase the chances of breakage and injure the watch.

DON'T use a mainspring that is too wide, and be sure that the tip and brace do not extend beyond the limits of the cover and barrel.

DON'T forget that a mainspring should not occupy more than one-third the diameter of the barrel, thus leaving two-thirds to be divided between the arbor and winding space, to enable the watch to run about 36 hours.

DON'T expect a mainspring to be flat if you put it in the barrel with the fingers. This method usually injures the spring, gives it a conical form, and thereby increases the friction in the barrel.

DON'T bend the inner or outer end of the mainspring with flat-nosed pliers, but provide yourself with specially made round-nosed pliers which will give a circular form to these parts, prevent short bends, contract the inner coil, and thus secure a closer fit to the barrel arbor without injuring the spring.

DON'T expect other than a properly fitted flat mainspring with rounded edges to produce the least friction in the barrel, allow the greatest amount of power to the train, and give the best results as to time, service, etc.

DON'T expect a mainspring to always endure extreme changes in temperature, or electrical disturbances, or straightening at full length, or neglect from lack of cleaning and oiling.

DON'T expect a watch that needs cleaning or other repairs to run satisfactorily by merely putting in a new mainspring.

DON'T expect a mainspring to plough through too much dirt.

CHAPTER XVII

WATCH RATE RECORDERS

THE Recorder consists of two units: the Recorder, which gives the written record of watch performance; and the frequency generator, which produces a standard frequency precise to 1 part in 100,000, or a continuous accuracy of less than 1 second per day deviation.

How the Recorder Works.—The standard frequency output of the generator drives a synchronous motor which rotates the drum of the Recorder at a uniform rate of 1 revolution per beat of a correct 5-beat watch. The watch to be tested is clamped in a spring mounting which can be rotated to give readings of the watch in various positions. The mechanical vibrations in the case, due to the escapement impact, are transmitted through a special pick-up and amplifier, and the amplified tick of the watch operates a recording stylus. This stylus is mounted under the drum, and travels the length of the drum actuated by a lead screw.

Chart paper is wrapped around the drum, fed from a roll inside the drum, and the markings are made on the paper by the stylus through a carbon ribbon. If a watch is exactly correct, its tick will repeat once every revolution of the drum, and as the stylus traverses the width of the record, a line of dots will be drawn which is parallel to the markings on the chart paper.

If the watch is fast, each tick will come slightly in advance of the one before it, since the drum is rotating at exactly the standard rate, and the result will be an upward-sloping line of dots. If the watch is slow, the line slopes downward. The paper is so calibrated that the slope of the record can be read in seconds per day.

The operation of making a measurement is very simple. The watch is clamped in the holder, set in the desired position, and the machine is started by a single motion of the handle on the front of the Recorder. The machine stops automatically when the record is completed.

Reading the Rate.—The time of the measurement is determined by the speed of the lead screw. Two speeds are available through a selective gear shift. Either a 5-second or a

Fig. 137.—The Western watch rate recorder.

Fig. 138.—Western recorde. with cover removed, showing vacuum tube amplifier which controls the recording stylus.

30-second measurement may be made. The 5-second record, for rough timing, gives a readable accuracy of 15 seconds per day. The 30-second recorder, being 6 times as long, shows a greater cumulative error in the watch, hence it is readable to 2 seconds per day. The machine makes an extremely flexible tool in the repair shop. Its major task is analysis of watch performance. Only short experience is required to become proficient in the simple procedure. Position error, isochronous error, and general average rate can be determined by the machine. In addition, such faults as banking, low-motion effect, loose pallet jewels, escape wheel eccentricity or tooth roughness, and other escapement troubles, draw distinctive records which immediately identify them.

When the fault is corrected, the machine permits a quick verification of the repair, and complete regulation within a few minutes.

Although the machine is designed primarily for 5-beat watches, it will also measure the rate of any beat train, faster or slower than 10,000 beats per hour. The rating of a 21,600 or 19,800 beat movement is as simple as an 18,000 movement.

Besides rating watches, the Recorder will time alarm clocks, automobile clocks, time recorders and meters, and other quick train movements which are too large to mount on the holder. This is done by simply clipping a wire from the object to be tested to the watch-holder of the machine; the sensitivity is such that the vibration transmitted through the wire will operate the machine. Hairsprings may also be vibrated by means of the Recorder. Another feature is a headphone jack which enables the jeweller to hear the amplified tick of the watch. This often proves a valuable aid in locating trouble.

The next chapter considers all types of watch rate recorders in greater detail.

CHAPTER XVIII

OTHER WATCH TESTING MACHINES

DURING the past few years, there have been produced many excellent machines which will record in a short time the rate of the watch—that is to say, whether it is gaining or losing. These machines are coming into general use, for they greatly speed-up the process of bringing a watch to time. They are, indeed, a practical necessity when making precision adjustments. Formerly, it was necessary to make a particular adjustment and to let the watch run for a day before the result of the adjustment could be observed. It is well-known that most watches have a gaining rate when fully wound which is compensated for by a losing rate when the watch is nearly run down. Thus the gaining and losing errors may in most cases balance out. The timer's job is to so adjust the overcoil of a hairspring that the watch has an even rate irrespective of whether the spring is fully-wound, half-wound, or nearly unwound. In other words, the watchmaker endeavours to shorten the long arcs, and lengthen the short arcs. The principles of these watch-testing machines were explained in a lecture given by Dr. A. W. Krause to the British Horological Institute. These machines provide a means of producing standard time against which to measure and make the watch signal its performance from the escapement and not as under the old system, by means of the hands. I summarise Dr. Krause's lecture for the benefit of those watchmakers who wish to install such a machine, which, if exhibited in the window with a notice inviting the public to have their watches tested, attracts considerable attention and custom.

"It is somewhat curious that anyone from the domain of physics should show the watchmaker how to improve his product; improvements in any field are usually devised by men working in the same or similar fields. Actually, the fundamentals of the apparatus to be described are due to modern physics.

Developments of this kind are made possible only by the high state of perfection of the various components used in so complex an apparatus. Briefly, I will cite the radio valve, without which this apparatus could never have been constructed. Then, since I am particularly interested in the quartz-operated machine, I must mention the brothers Curie, who, in 1885, discovered 'piezo-electricity', i.e., the principle that when pressure is applied to certain substances such as quartz, a small voltage is developed. Later we shall see the importance of this property of quartz.

It is preferable to regard these machines as timepiece analysers, and to classify them as follows:

A. *Subjective or Recording Analysers.*
  1. Integrating Systems (Siemens-Straumann).
  2. Differentiating Systems (Western, Gibbs).
B. *Objective Analysers.*
  1. Acoustical (sound amplifier).
  2. Optical (stroboscope, cathode ray tube).

The fundamental components of all these analysers are: (1) Microphone; (2) Amplifier; (3) Indicator or Recorder; (4) Time Standard, which may be a good watch or clock of known rate, or any other timepiece of suitable accuracy, of low or high frequency.

Subjective Analysers: Integrating System (Siemens-Straumann).—This system, known as the 'time-balance', records the tick of the watch under test by means of a conventional, but highly damped recording voltmeter. The recording paper is motor-driven, at speeds which are adjustable within wide limits, to provide either quick readings or extended readings of greater accuracy. Energising impulses from the master and from the watch under test are fed through separate amplifiers and thyratrons to a pair of coils, placed 180° apart, in the recording instrument. The system records the phase relation between the tested watch and the master. When the two are in step, the graph shows a straight line; the gain or loss of the tested watch being indicated by a deviation to right or left. The graph is a continuous line and its irregularities reveal to a trained observer any defects in the watch.

The value of this apparatus has been enhanced by the special master used as a time-base. This consists of a seconds pendulum which, by means of a photo-electric cell and amplifier, holds in step a one-fifth seconds pendulum against which the tested watch is compared.

Differentiating Systems (Western Electric).—The time-standard employed here is a 300-cycle tuning fork which excites two coils and, through an amplifier, drives a synchronous motor. The motor shaft rotates 5 times per second and carries a drum 2 in. in diameter, to which is fixed the recording paper. The motor also causes a stylus to traverse the paper in a direction parallel to the axis of the drum. Each tick of the tested watch passes through a microphone and amplifier, and brings the stylus momentarily into contact with the paper. The succession of ticks produce a series of marks as the stylus traverses the drum. Marks proceeding horizontally across the chart indicate that the watch is keeping correct time, rise or fall showing gain or loss, as explained in the previous chapter.

The drum is stopped after each test for the chart to be read and changed. The drive for the stylus traverse is provided with two ratios to give either quick readings in 5 seconds or more accurate readings in 30 seconds. One division on the chart indicates an error of 5 seconds per day on a 30-second observation. Defects in the watch are shown as irregularities in the line of marks.

The tuning fork is of a special alloy and is enclosed in a thermostatically controlled temperature chamber to maintain a closely constant frequency.

Gibbs.—The Gibbs 'Time Micrometer' uses a quartz clock as time-standard. The basis of this is a quartz crystal vibrating 108,000 times a second. The accuracy of this frequency is 10^{-7}, or 1 in 10,000,000 and, allowing for mechanical and other factors of the complete apparatus, permits readings to an accuracy of $\frac{1}{80}$ second per day. I have previously mentioned the discovery by the brothers Curie that quartz has the property of generating a small voltage when subject to pressure. This process can be reversed, and an alternating voltage of predetermined frequency applied to the crystal causes the latter to vibrate physically. Quartz will vibrate only at its own natural frequency, which is governed by its dimensions and, to some extent, by temperature. A valve oscillator, tuned closely to the frequency of the crystal, is used to provide power. The crystal is connected in the grid circuit of this valve and, on commencing to vibrate, takes control of the frequency of oscillation.

The quartz crystal measures $30 \times 18 \times 2 \cdot 2$ mm., these dimensions giving a frequency of 108,000 cycles per second. The effect of temperature is used to perform the same function as the regulator of a watch; it is the 'fine-setting' control. The crystal is enclosed in a temperature chamber maintained at 52°C.+12°C., by means of a bi-metallic thermostatic strip 62 cm. in length.

The frequency of 108,000 cycles per second is too high to operate any mechanical device such as a motor or clock, and must therefore, be reduced to practical dimensions. This necessitates a device known as a multivibrator or de-multiplier, which reduces the frequency from 108,000 to 60 cycles per second. This is achieved by successive valve stages with resistance-capacity circuits operating on the principle of trigger action.

The quartz-controlled 60-cycle current leaves the last stage of the de-multiplier in saw-tooth form, and is then converted to a sine wave of 70 volts, part of which is fed to a valve giving an output of 3 watts at 110 volts. This voltage is used to operate a 60-cycle synchronous clock, which by astronomical or other comparison proves an exact check on the accuracy of the crystal.

For the observation of watches, part of the 70-volt sine wave is fed to the driver valve, which in turn affects the grids of 4-power amplifier valves, each having an output of 18 watts. From the frequency generator unit we derive, therefore, 72 watts of quartz controlled power. This is used to drive a 40-watt self-starting synchronous motor of special design, which serves as the actual time-base of the recorder unit. The motor has a constant speed of 30 turns per second, which is reduced by gearing to 5 per second on a shaft carrying 2 aluminium discs, each 144 mm. in diameter. One disc has on its periphery 11 teeth, and the other 12 teeth. These teeth produce the markings on the recorder paper and have the high writing speed of 2,255 mm. per second.

The paper is equal in width to the distance between 2 teeth on the 11-tooth disc, so that one tooth of each disc is always under the paper. The synchronous motor also feeds the recorder paper, at a speed of 6 in. per minute. Either disc may be used for recording 5-beat watches; the 11-tooth disc is used for 5½-beat, and the 12-tooth for 6-beat escapements. A selector knob on the front of the unit determines which disc is in operation.

The watch under test provides impulse by way of a 'Piezo-Electric' microphone, amplifier and armature, to a printer bar situated on top of the paper and exactly above the edge of the disc in use. Between the paper and the printing bar is a carbon ribbon such as is used in typewriters. Each tick of the watch pulls down the printer bar, which presses the ribbon and paper on to a tooth of the disc below and a mark is made on the paper. This mark may be anywhere on the paper beneath the printing bar, according to the position of the marking tooth at the instant of contact. If the watch is keeping perfect time, marks will appear in a vertical line. If it is losing, they will slope to the left; if gaining, to the right.

The 'Piezo-Electric' microphone is of special design and is rotatory to permit observation of watches in different positions. The accuracy of the machine and the high writing speed of the discs show up small irregularities in the watch to the order of $\frac{1}{2000}$ second. This is useful for analysis of troubles of various origin, such as bad poise, eccentric wheels or faulty tooth engagement in the train of a watch.

For use in factories where extreme accuracy is not essential and speed of operation is important, a movable dial placed over the paper and an indicator showing the angle of slope of the line of marks enable the angle to be read off as error in seconds per day. Readings accurate to 2 seconds per day can thus be made very quickly, and unprinted paper used in the recorder.

The whole machine is unaffected by minor variations of voltage and frequency in the supply mains.

Objective Analysers (Acoustical).—The acoustical analyser, consisting of microphone, amplifier and loud-speaker or earphones, is the most elementary of this group. It is preferable to employ a contact microphone which picks up mechanical vibrations induced in the watchcase, by the action of the escapement, rather than sound vibrations transmitted through air. The type of microphone here demonstrated consists of a Rochelle salt crystal, fastened on three corners and the fourth carrying a stylus. The vibrations transmitted by the stylus stress the crystal and produce a small voltage, of the order of 8 mv., from a pocket watch. This voltage is amplified and operates a loud-speaker. With experience, some watchmakers have developed considerable ability in detecting many types of error by this system.

Optical Analysers.—First, we have the stroboscope machines, and there are represented here instruments of two different types: (1) the French, due to Lepaute; and (2) the American, due to Normann, of Chicago, and marketed in the U.S.A. under the name Paulson.

The French Machine.—This machine has two microphones, two amplifiers, a stroboscope disc, and requires as time-base a master watch of known rate. The stroboscope motor is a

Ferraris disc driven by the mains, the speed being adjustable within fine limits. The top of the motor axis carries a black hand. Behind the hand is a white translucent disc, and behind that a circular neon tube. In front of the hand is another disc, 4 in. in diameter, transparent, bearing a scale marked in divisions each of $\frac{1}{100}$ second. To the axis of the motor is also fixed an armature which passes through the field of a corrector coil energised by amplified impulses from the master watch.

In operation, the motor is started and its speed adjusted to 301 or 302 revolutions per minute in the case of a master watch beating $\frac{1}{5}$ second. The motor and its hand thus turn a trifle more than one revolution in the time of one beat of the watch. The amplified impulses from the master watch are fed to the corrector coil, which acts on the armature to synchronise each revolution of the hand with one beat of the master watch.

The watch to be tested is then placed on the microphone of the second amplifier and each beat of its escapement causes a flash of the neon tube which shows up the instantaneous position of the hand driven by the motor. If the hand appears stationary in successive flashes, then the tested watch is going at the same rate as the master, but if it appears to drift in either direction the tested watch is gaining or losing as compared with the master. Anti-clockwise drift of one complete division on the scale ($\frac{1}{100}$ second) during an observation of 1 minute duration indicates that the tested watch is gaining 14·4 seconds per day.

American Stroboscope Machines have some similarity with the French machine, the principal differences being in the drive and correcting methods. Each of the American machines is driven by a synchronous motor running in step with the alternating current of the supply mains. The speed of the motor is liable to vary slightly, corresponding to variations of the load on the mains, so a master watch is again used to correct these variations of speed. The motor is designed to rotate one turn per second, and mounted on its shaft by a friction clutch are a 5-pole corrector armature and a celluloid disc. The armature and disc are rigidly mounted in relation to each other, but together can move with some freedom in relation to the motor shaft. The main synchronous rotor is fixed rigidly on the shaft. Surrounding the corrector armature is a stationary 5-pole field energised by amplified impulses from the master watch. When a variation of the mains

frequency causes a difference in phase between the armature
and stationary poles of the correcting device an impulse from
the master watch overcomes the friction of the clutch and
pulls the armature and the disc into step with the master.

At the beginning of a test a movable hand mounted on the
front of the case is set against the visible zero on the disc as
shown by the neon flashes. After an observation of 1 minute
the drift is read off against the hand in seconds per day gain
or loss according to direction.

Cathode Ray Indicators.—Two types of cathode ray oscillo-
scopes have been developed for testing watches—the rectangular and the polar co-ordinate systems. In the rectangular
system, the phase difference between the master and test
watches is shown by motion of the pattern across the screen
of the tube.

In the polar co-ordinate system the motion is shown in a
circle, which is better adapted to the shape of the screen in the
cathode ray tube and permits closer reading. Incidentally,
this system is being used for the precise tuning of musical
instruments in an American factory. For testing watches the
sonic frequencies generated by the tick of the escapement
are passed through filters, each range of frequency being
represented by one dot in a circle of dots produced on the
screen. The number of dots as well as their rotation indicate
the condition of the watch under test.

In both systems a standard time-base in the form of a good
chronometer or pendulum clock is used, and drift of the
pattern in one direction or other indicates if the watch is
gaining or losing.

The Gibbs Hairspring Vibrator.—Since the fundamental
system of the quartz clock is an extremely accurate time-base,
many other applications will suggest themselves. One recent
application and the use of another new electronic device
enables the vibrating of hairsprings to be carried out with an
accuracy and speed of operation hitherto unknown. The
quartz frequency generator supplies a synchronous motor
driving a visual indicator in the form of a stroboscope. The
hairspring and balance wheel is placed in the holder and set in
motion. On the rim of the balance wheel is concentrated a
small beam of light, part of which is reflected into a photo-
electric cell. As long as the balance wheel is in motion, a
certain intensity of light is maintained in the photo-cell.
Due to a physical function of the metal of the balance wheel

a change occurs in the intensity of the light reflected into the photo-cell at the instant the balance is at rest. This is used to flash two rotating lamps behind the large stroboscope dial, and indicates the period of the balance swing. The dial is

Fig. 139a.—An enlarged view of a modern wrist-watch movement.

divided into two sections, indicating fast and slow. In effect, the operator observes an electrically magnified image of the balance wheel, and increased speed and accuracy with less fatigue are obtained by this method."

CHAPTER XIX

THE N.P.L. WATCH TESTS

VERY few people understand what is meant by an accurate watch. They read advertisements of watch manufacturers who describe their products as accurate timekeepers, correct timekeepers, good timekeepers, excellent timekeepers, precise timekeepers, fine timekeepers, and so on. Whilst these terms may be correct up to a point, they do not convey anything to

Fig. 140.—In order to pass the Kew "A" test, every part of the escapement must receive attention. Position errors must be eliminated, the balance must be in poise, and the pivots in perfect condition.

a horologist, for one manufacturer may consider a rate of 30 seconds a day as "accurate," or "correct," or "precise," but unless we know what is considered the standard of good timekeeping these terms do not give any indication of the performance of the watch. Now that we have the time signal radiated from Greenwich at regular periods each day, the public has formed the habit of checking the rates of watches and clocks, and it finds that what was formerly thought to be a good timepiece is inaccurate. But providing that a watch has a constant rate—either gaining or losing, it is easy to estimate the time from the indication given by the hands, for the hands merely indicate the rate of a watch. The speed of movement of the hands is governed by the vibration of the hairspring attached to the balance of the watch, and its ability to keep time depends upon the accuracy of the balance, the quality of the pivots and the jewels, the hairspring, and the poising of the balance.

Not only must the watch have a constant rate, but it must have a constant rate in all positions. Obviously some impartial body must be set the task of testing the claims of manufacturers to label their watches as accurate timekeepers, and to set the standard by which watches may be judged. In this country that body is the National Physical Laboratory at Teddington, who issue Certificates under certain conditions of performance. It is very necessary that official timekeepers and others concerned with the accurate checking and recording of the passage of time, including the captains of ships, should possess watches known to be accurate. A record can be gained by a fifth of a second, and if the record was timed by a watch which could gain that amount in an hour, the record has been wrongly recorded.

The Metrology Department (rating division), undertakes the tests of watches submitted to them. There are two classes of test— A and B, which occupy 45 and 31 days respectively. The Class "A" test is divided into 8 periods:

Period	Approximate Temperature	Position of Watch
1.	67°F.	In the "initial" vertical position (*see note below*).
2.	67°F.	In a vertical position, turned clockwise through 90° from the "initial" position.
3.	67°F.	In a vertical position, turned anti-clockwise through 90° from the "initial" position.
4.	42°F.	In a horizontal position, with dial up.
5.	67°F.	In a horizontal position, with dial up.
6.	92°F.	In a horizontal position, with dial up.
7.	67°F.	In a horizontal position, with dial down.
8.	67°F.	In the "initial" vertical position.

For the purpose of this test the "initial" vertical position is defined as follows: Pendant uppermost, in the case of pendant watches; 6 (VI) o'clock uppermost, in the case of wristlet watches; 12 (XII) o'clock uppermost in the case of other watches not intended for pendant or wristlet use.

Periods 1, 2, 3, and 8, consist of 5 days each, but the remaining periods, 4, 5, 6, and 7, each occupy 6 days, as owing to intervening changes in temperature, the rate obtained on the first day of each of these 4 periods is not used for the purpose of the test.

Class "A" certificates are issued for watches whose performance was such that: the numerical average of the daily departures from the mean daily rate, during any one of the 8 periods of test, did not exceed 2 seconds; the mean daily rate in the "initial" vertical position (see note later on), differed from that in the "dial up" position at 67°F. by less than 5 seconds, and from that in any other position by less than 10 seconds; the mean change of daily rate with change of temperature was less than 0·3 seconds per 1°F. The mean daily rate did not exceed 10 seconds in any position (i.e. in any one of Periods 1, 2, 3, 5, 7 and 8).

The certificate is endorsed with the words "especially good" when a watch obtains a total of 80 marks or more out of a maximum of 100.

Subsidiary Class "A" Test.—A watch which has previously obtained a Class "A" certificate may be entered for a subsidiary re-test normally occupying 8 days. The watch is tested in the same positions and temperatures as those prescribed for Class "A," and the original certificate is endorsed with the date of the re-test if the watch is found to be performing within Class "A" limits.

Class "B."—This test occupies 5 periods as follows:

Period	Duration	Approximate Temperature	Position of Watch
1.	14 days	67°F.	Watch in a vertical position (*see note below*).
2.	14 days	67°F.	Watch in a horizontal position.
3.	1 day	42°F.	Watch in a horizontal position.
4.	1 day	67°F.	Watch in a horizontal position.
5.	1 day	92°F.	Watch in a horizontal position.

The National Physical Laboratory

RATING DEPARTMENT

I hereby Certify

That a CLASS **A** KEW CERTIFICATE

has been issued to   Mr. F. J. Camm,

London,

for the keyless   open-face   "Solvil"   pocket   watch

No. ---739748--- , which was submitted to a test at this

Institution from   1st April to 16th May, 1939,

and the results of its performance were such as to entitle it to this

Certificate, in accordance with the Regulations for the issue of

Watch-rate Certificates, approved by The National Physical Laboratory

Committee of the Royal Society.

C. G. Darwin

DIRECTOR

Figs. 140a & 141. Reproductions of the Kew "A" Certificate issued to the author of this book, who succeeded in obtaining 78 marks. A watch which only just passes the test receives none of these marks.

RESULTS OF TEST OF WATCH No. ---739748---

Rated from   1st April to 15th May, 1939.

Period	Approximate Temperature	Position of Watch	Mean Rate. Seconds per day
1	67°F.	In the "initial" vertical position (see note on opposite page)	+1.2
2	67°F.	In a vertical position, turned clockwise through 90° from the "initial" position	+6.1
3	67°F.	In a vertical position, turned anticlockwise through 90° from the "initial" position	-6.0
4	42°F.	In a horizontal position, with dial up	-2.5
5	67°F.	,, ,, ,, ,, ,, ,,	+0.2
6	92°F.	,, ,, ,, ,, ,, ,,	+1.8
7	67°F.	In a horizontal position, with dial down	-2.4
8	67°F.	In the "initial" vertical position	-1.9

Mean variation of rate (average for all periods)............0.20....sec. per day

Mean change of rate per 1° Faht..............0.090....,,   ,,

Maximum difference between any two
individual rates during the test ....13.0..........,,   ,,

Note: + gaining   — losing

MARKS AWARDED

In respect of consistency of rate.............................35.9

,,   ,,   constancy of rate with change of position..............28.1

,,   ,,   temperature compensation...........................14.0

TOTAL MARKS   78.0

CLASS A CERTIFICATE ISSUED

Date: 19th May, 1939.

J M Burch
Observer

C G Darwin
Director

Reference: 23775.

Fig. 141.

For the purpose of this test the "vertical position" is defined as follows: Pendant uppermost, in the case of pendant watches; 6 (VI) o'clock uppermost, in the case of wristlet watches; 12 (XII) o'clock uppermost, in the case of other watches not intended for pendant or wristlet use.

Class "B" certificates are issued for watches whose performance was such that: the numerical average of the daily departures from the mean daily rate during the same period of test did not exceed 2 seconds in either Period 1 or Period 2; the mean daily rate in Period 1 differed from that in Period 2 by less than 10 seconds; the mean daily rate did not exceed 15 seconds in either Period 1 or Period 2; the mean change of daily rate with change of temperature was less than 0·3 seconds per 1°F.

The certificate is endorsed with the words "especially good" when the mean variation of daily rate did not exceed 0·75 seconds for the average of Periods 1 and 2 taken separately, when the difference between the mean daily rate in pendant up and dial up positions was less than 5 seconds, and when the mean change of daily rate with change of temperature was less than 0·2 seconds per 1°F.

Chronograph Watches.—Each chronograph watch entered for Class "A" or Class "B" is first tested for the action of its chronograph mechanism.

The ordinary Class "A," Subsidary "A" or Class "B" test, which is made with the chronograph mechanism disengaged, is not commenced unless the watch is found satisfactory as regards the chronograph action.

The following are the particulars and conditions of the tests made on the chronograph action.

If the watch fails to comply with these conditions, or is otherwise unsatisfactory, it will be rejected without any further test.

Tests are made over one or more periods of 24 hours each at about 67°F. in the "dial up" position: (a) with the chronograph disengaged; (b) with the chronograph in action; and (c) in the case of a split-seconds chronograph with the hands split.

The daily rate found under (b) must not differ by more than 5 seconds from that found under (a) or (c).

Short Tests.—(a) When the chronograph mechanism is in action and pressure is applied to the push-piece, the chronograph hand or hands must either stop dead at once, or else they must run on unaffected until stronger force is used; (b) there must be complete absence of "lagging" and moving in "spasmodic" jumps when pressure is applied to the push-piece; (c) the chronograph hand must start exactly from, and return to, the zero mark. The inclusive errors of starting and stopping must not exceed $\pm \frac{1}{5}$ second. In the case of a split-seconds chronograph, the hands must run together in exact accordance unless split; (d) the indications of the minute-recorder must be exactly consistent with the position of the chronograph hand. In the case of "instantaneous" and "semi-instantaneous" minute-recorders, if the chronograph hand is stopped at $59\frac{1}{2}$ seconds, the minute-recorder should not indicate the completion of 1 minute. Conversely, if the chronograph hand is stopped at $60\frac{1}{2}$ seconds, the recorder must not fail to indicate the completion of 1 minute.

Basis of Computation of the Marks Awarded.—Each Class "A" certificate issued for a watch will contain a statement of the marks awarded on the results of the complete test.

Marks are assessed for:

(1) Consistency of daily rate. (Maximum = 40 marks).
(2) Position adjustment. (Maximum = 40 marks).
(3) Temperature compensation. (Maximum = 20 marks).

The certificate is endorsed with the words "especially good" when a watch obtains a total of 80 marks or more out of a maximum of 100.

Consistency of Daily Rate.—The numerical average of the departures of the individual daily rates from the mean daily rate for a given period of test, is defined as the "mean variation of daily rate" for that period.

The final value, in seconds, obtained for the "mean variation of daily rate" is the numerical average of the 8 individual values of the "mean variation of daily rate," obtained separately for the 8 different periods of the test.

Marks awarded for consistency of daily rate:

$$= 40\left(1 - \frac{a}{2}\right)$$

Position Adjustment.—The marks awarded for position adjustment are computed entirely on the results of the 6 periods, Nos. 1, 2, 3, 5, 7, and 8, in which the test is made with the watch in different positions, at the normal temperature of 67°F.

The mean variation of rate with change of position, (b) in

seconds, is taken as the numerical average of the departures of the 6 mean values of the daily rate in Periods Nos. 1, 2, 3, 5, 7, and 8, from the algebraic mean of the 6 mean values.

Marks awarded for position adjustment:

$$= 40 \left(1 - \frac{b}{10} \right)$$

Temperature Compensation.—The marks awarded for temperature compensation are computed on the results of Periods Nos. 4, 5, and 6. These portions of the test are made in the "dial up" position and relate to temperatures measured in Fahrenheit degrees.

The temperature coefficient, (c) in seconds per $1°F.$, that is, the mean change of daily rate for a change in temperature of $1°F.$, is defined by the following ratio:

$$c = \frac{\text{The sum of the numerical departures of the 3 average daily rates in Periods 4, 5, and 6, from the algebraic mean of these 3 average daily rates.}}{\text{The sum of the numerical departures of the 3 mean temperatures in Periods 4, 5, and 6, from the average temperatures for these 3 periods.}}$$

Marks awarded for temperature compensation:

$$= 20 \left(1 - \frac{10c}{3} \right)$$

The total marks awarded are therefore obtainable from the following formula:

$$\text{Total marks} = 40 \left(1 - \frac{a}{2} \right) + 40 \left(1 - \frac{b}{10} \right) + 20 \left(1 - \frac{10c}{3} \right)$$

Where a is the final value of the mean variation of daily rate (average for all 8 periods of test), b is the mean variation of rate with change of position (Periods 1, 2, 3, 5, 7, and 8), c is the mean change of daily rate per $1°F.$

CHAPTER XX

RATING A WATCH FOR A KEW CERTIFICATE

The A test is severe, and the margin of error has to be small. The general layout of the movement has to be carefully studied—the hardness of the jewels, the correct gearing of the wheels, the action of the mainspring and the function of the escapement. Changes of temperature will naturally cause a variation in the size of the watch in general (of course, very minute), but the greatest effect will take place in the balance and balance spring.

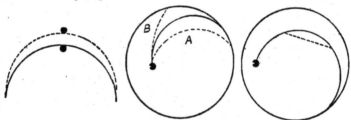

Fig. 142.—A losing rate is caused by the hairspring beating against two pins as shown.

Fig. 143.—The short arcs are slow at A and fast at B.

Fig. 144.—Some adjusters make an inward bend in the overcoil as shown.

The Balance.—Before submitting a watch to even preliminary tests, it is essential that the balance be correctly poised. In other words, that the weight of the balance be evenly distributed. The fact that a balance is heavy at one point will have no effect upon its going when in a horizontal position. When tested in a vertical position there will be a decided gaining or losing according to the position of the error.

For example, assume a watch "pendant up" vertical position 12 o'clock uppermost, with the balance at rest. If the heaviest point is at the bottom, the balance will go slow if its vibration is less than a turn. If the heaviest point was at the top the result would be reversed. Some ordinary grade watches which are only timed in two positions have the balance purposely thrown out of poise to create a slight gaining rate in the "pendant up" position, an effective but very undesirable practice as the watch would be quite unreliable in any other vertical position. From the foregoing it will be seen that the slightest error will affect the timekeeping.

Chamfering sinks in the underside of the balance rim or the use of the file both detract from the appearance of the balance. The neatest way is to cut the slots of the temperature screws deeper. The quarter screws should never be touched, but always left the same distance from the rim. (A poising tool was described earlier.) Not until a balance is perfectly poised should any attempt be made with timing.

A Losing Rate.—There should be no play between the index pins of the regulator, but just sufficient freedom for the regulator to move without kinking the spring. With a wide gap, considerable variation will take place during the long and short vibrations of the balance. If during the short vibrations the hairspring is stationary on one pin or beating slightly on one pin, it is more than probable that the spring will beat against the two pins during the long vibrations and so cause a losing rate. (See Fig. 142.)

Now that the balance is perfectly poised, preliminary tests can be made in different temperatures, and adjustment made by altering the position of some of the temperature screws. The centre bar of a brass and steel balance is made of steel. Therefore, during an increase of temperature the screws near this bar will move slightly outwards. The cut or free ends, however, together with their screws, will move inwards. There is, however, a middle position in which certain screws remain at the same distance from the centre.

Should a watch gain in heat, it will be necessary to move one or more screws from the free ends towards the fixed ends. If during a higher temperature a loss is experienced, screws will have to be moved from the fixed ends towards the free ends. Under no circumstances must screws be moved except in pairs, in order to retain the poise of the balance. After temperature tests the screws in the unaffected area may be used for mean time adjustment.

Temperature Changes.—Preliminary positional tests can be made after corrections have been made for temperature changes. Change of position has its effect upon the action of the escapement and in many instances pivot friction is increased. The rate, that is the time of vibration of the balance, must be uniform as the mainspring gradually runs down, as it must also be in various positions. Isochronism, the performance of the vibrations of the balance in the same time in both the long arcs and the short arcs, is therefore of prime importance.

A "dial up" position usually represents the long arcs, and the vertical positions the short arcs. To test for isochronism the mainspring should be wound about one turn and the watch placed in a vertical position, as this will produce the shortest possible vibration. The watch should be set and the subsequent gain or loss noted. A test in the horizontal position with the mainspring fully wound will produce the longest vibration. The gain or loss should be noted.

Positional Errors.—Positional errors may be due to a multitude of causes—escapement faults, excessive friction in balance jewel holes, damaged jewels, uneven end jewels, or careless oiling. Often the sides of the lever and the banking pins become so sticky as to retard the action. A little friction may take place between the fork and the roller. A ruby pin very slightly out of upright may rub the fork as it passes in and out in certain positions. Should there be an error in one vertical position only, or should the error in one vertical position be greatly in excess of the other vertical positions, the trouble will probably be traced to a defective jewel hole. The only cure for a jewel hole showing the slightest imperfection is to replace it with a new jewel hole.

If the escapement appears to be in order, but the long and short arcs are still not isochronous, it will be necessary to alter the overcoil of the hairspring. If the short arcs are slow, the overcoil is bent inwards, at the same time forming a little more of the body of the spring into the overcoil as at A in Fig. 143.

When the short arcs are fast the overcoil is made less curved as at B in Fig. 143. Some adjusters make an inward curve in the overcoil, as shown in Fig. 144 when the short arcs are slow. Special curved Breguet spring tweezers should be used, as any undue kinking will be almost certain to upset the timekeeping.

Reducing Vibration.—A method sometimes used to reduce the vibration in the long arcs is to flatten the end of the balance pivot with an oilstone slip. This will increase the friction in the horizontal position, thereby making the long and short arcs of the same duration. There is, unfortunately, a possibility that the pivot so treated may cause wear in the endstone. An alternative method would be to reduce the size of the balance

	1	2	3	4	5	6	7
1	1—6	Pendant up	68·30	+1·61 +1·73 +1·61 +1·63 +1·61	+1·63	0·02 0·10 0·02 0·00 0·02	0·032
2	6—11	Pendant right	68·40		+1·95		0·091
3	11—16	Pendant left	67·80		+1·73		0·114
4	17—22	Dial up	42·15		+1·57		0·101
5	23—28	Dial up	67·76		+1·66		0·033
6	29—34	Dial up	94·70		+2·00		0·095
7	35—40	Dial down	67·77		+1·93		0·040
8	40—45	Pendant up	67·65		+1·90		0·061

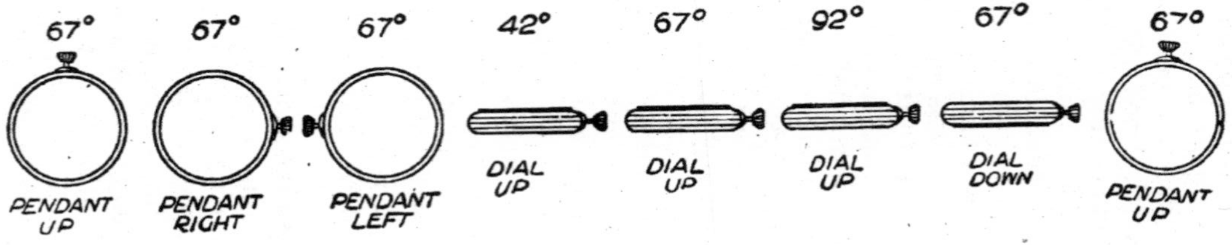

Fig. 145.— The eight testing positions of a watch during the Kew test; to the right is shown a specimen table of results of a watch undergoing a test.

67° PENDANT UP   67° PENDANT RIGHT   67° PENDANT LEFT   42° DIAL UP   67° DIAL UP   92° DIAL UP   67° DIAL DOWN   67° PENDANT UP pivot and fit a smaller and thinner jewel hole, thereby reducing the friction in the vertical position to a minimum. Adjustment of the contact between hairspring and regulator pins, although not a desirable practice, can be effective. The hairspring is adjusted to remain on one pin in vertical positions, but to vibrate between both pins in horizontal positions.

From the foregoing it will be realised that considerable fine adjustment is necessary if a watch is to occupy a high position in the award list.

Fig. 145 shows a specimen table of results of a watch undergoing a test. Column 1 indicates the period, column 2 the various positions, column 3 the different temperatures, whilst the remaining columns show the various errors in timekeeping. In column 4 is shown the rate per day in seconds per day on each of the five days of the first period (actually the figures show a slight gain). From these daily rates is computed the "mean daily rate". The "mean daily rate" is, of course, the average of the 5 daily rates. The first figure in column 5 represents the "mean daily rate" for the first period, the other figures represent the "mean daily rate" for the other 7 periods.

"Daily Variation".—Column 6 shows the "daily variation from the mean rate" for the first period. These figures are obtained by subtracting the individual daily rates from the "mean daily rate". The "mean daily variation of the rate for the period" is shown in column 7. This value is obtained by adding up the "daily variations from the mean rate" and dividing by 5. The mean values for the other periods are obtained in the same way. For the purpose of allocating marks for position adjustment the 6 positions at the normal temperature are considered, viz., periods 1, 2, 3, 5, 7, 8. For temperature compensation only the periods 4, 5, 6, are used, but the average of the 8 "mean variations of daily rate" forms the basis for deciding the consistency of daily rate.

To obtain an "A" certificate the change of daily rate with change of temperature must be less than 0·3 seconds per 1°F. the mean daily rate must not be more than 10 seconds; the mean variation of daily rate must not be more than 2 seconds in any of the 8 periods; pendant up and dial up positions must not differ by more than 5 seconds; 10 seconds between pendant up and any other position. To obtain full 100 marks (20 marks for temperature compensation, 40 marks for position adjustment, and 40 marks for consistency of daily rate), a watch would have no temperature error, its rate would be constant and unaffected by change of position.

As already stated, the formula used to determine the marks is:

$$40 \left(1 - \frac{a}{2}\right) + 40 \left(1 - \frac{b}{10}\right) + 20 \left(1 - \frac{10c}{3}\right)$$

a = mean variation of the daily rate for the whole 8 periods.

b = the mean variation with change of position (6 periods only).

c = the mean change of the daily rate for $1°$F.

The first part of the formula will be considered as an example viz., the consistency of daily rate $40 \left(1 - \frac{a}{2}\right)$ the average of all the results shown in column 7, Fig. 145 is 0·070. Substituting this result for a gives:

$$40 \left(1 - \frac{0·070}{2}\right) = 40 \left(1 - 0·035\right) = 40 \left(0·965\right) = 38·6.$$

38·6 marks out of a possible 40. By similar methods, the values of the other quantities b and c can be found. A watch with 80 or more marks is endorsed "especially good".

Basis of Marks.—As already stated, a maximum of 40 marks is allotted for consistency of rate, 40 for positional adjustment, and 20 for temperature compensation. The basis of computation of the marks actually awarded is set out below, the numerical data being taken from an example to be found on page 146.

For the sake of clarity the daily rates and much of the working in the examples are taken to the first place of decimals only. In the tests themselves the daily rates are determined to two decimal places and further decimal places are retained in the calculations until the final rounding to the nearest 0·1 of a mark.

Consistency of Daily Rate.—The consistency of the daily rate is observed throughout the test. In the example the daily rate during the first 5-day period varies from −3·9 to −4·3 secs. per day, the mean rate being −4·1 secs. per day.

For each day the departure of the actual rate from the mean rate of the period is tabulated, and in the example the average of the five departures in Period I is shown to be 0·16 secs. per day.

The results similarly obtained for each of the eight periods of test are:—

Period	I	II	III	IV	V	VI	VII	VIII
Average departure of rate from mean rate for period (secs. per day) ..	0·16	0·40	0·22	0·56	0·54	0·34	0·78	0·26
Grand mean variation of rate (a) ..	0·41 secs. per day.							

A maximum of 40 marks is allotted for consistency of daily rate. Watches showing no variation of rate in each position or temperature (i.e., grand mean variation of rate, a, = zero) would receive this marking. Marks are deducted in proportion to a, all 40 marks being deducted if the value of $a = 2$ secs. per day, which is equal to the maximum permissible variation of rate in any one period. Thus the marks awarded $= 40 - \dfrac{a}{2} \times 40$. The watch dealt with in the above example obtains $40 - \dfrac{0·41}{2} \times 40 = 31·8$ marks in respect of consistency of rate.

Constancy of Rate with Change of Position.—The marks awarded for positional adjustment are computed from the six mean rates obtained in Periods I, II, III, V, VII and VIII, in which the test is made with the watch in different positions at constant temperature, and the departures of these values from their grand mean determine the marks awarded, as follows:

Period	I	II	III	V	VII	VIII
Mean rate for period (secs. per day) ..	−4·1	−4·5	+2·1	−3·0	−1·3	−2·4
Grand mean ..	−2·2 secs. per day.					
Departure of above mean rates from grand mean (secs. per day)	1·9	2·3	4·3	0·8	0·9	0·2
Average departure, i.e., mean variation of rate with change of position (b) ..	1·73 secs. per day.					

A maximum of 40 marks is awarded for constancy of rate with change of position. Watches showing no change of rate with change of position (i.e., average departure, b secs. per day, = zero) would receive this marking. Marks are deducted, in proportion to b, at the rate of 4 marks for an average departure of 1 second, so that the marks awarded in respect of positional adjustment = $40 - 4b$. The watch dealt with in the above example obtains $40 - 4 \times 1 \cdot 73 = 33 \cdot 1$ marks in respect of positional adjustment.

Constancy of Rate with Change of Temperature.—The marks awarded for temperature compensation are computed from the three mean rates obtained in Periods IV, V and VI, in which the test is made with the watch in the same position but at different temperatures. Both the rates and the temperatures obtaining in the test are taken into account as follows:

Period	Rate (sec. per day)			Temperature (°F.)		
	IV	V	VI	IV	V	VI
Mean rate and temperature	$-0 \cdot 1$	$-3 \cdot 0$	$-0 \cdot 3$	$41 \cdot 6$	$66 \cdot 8$	$92 \cdot 0$
Grand mean ..	$-1 \cdot 1$ secs. per day.			$66 \cdot 8$°F.		
Departures from grand mean	$1 \cdot 0$	$1 \cdot 9$	$0 \cdot 8$	$25 \cdot 2$	$0 \cdot 0$	$25 \cdot 2$
Sum of departures ..	$3 \cdot 7$ secs. per day.			$50 \cdot 4$°F.		
Mean change of rate 1°F. change of temperature (c) ...	$3 \cdot 7 \div 50 \cdot 4 = 0 \cdot 073$ secs. per day.					

A maximum of 20 marks is allotted for constancy of rate with change of temperature. Watches showing no change of rate with change of temperature (i.e., c = zero) would receive this marking. Marks are deducted in proportion to c, all 20 marks being deducted if $c = 0 \cdot 3$ secs. per day per 1°F., the maximum value allowed, and thus the marks awarded $= 20 - \dfrac{c}{0 \cdot 3} \times 20$.

The watch dealt with in the above example obtains $20 - \dfrac{0 \cdot 073}{0 \cdot 3} \times 20 = 15 \cdot 1$ marks in respect of temperature compensation.

EXAMPLE OF THE DAILY PERFORMANCE OF A WATCH OBTAINING 60 MARKS IN THE CLASS A TEST

Days of Test.	Period and Nominal Temperature.	Position and Mean Temperature of Watch.	Daily Rate. (seconds per day).	Mean Rate for Period (seconds per day).	Daily Variation from Mean Rate (secs per day).	Mean Variation of Rate for Period (seconds per day).
1–6	Period I 67°F.	Pendant up 67·2°F.	+5·3 +6·9 +3·1 +2·5 +3·5	+4·3	1·0 2·6 1·2 1·8 0·8	1·48
6–11	Period II 67°F.	Pendant right 67·5°F.	−2·7 −3·7 −2·1 −3·3 −2·0	−2·8	0·1 0·9 0·7 0·5 0·8	0·60
11–16	Period III 67°F.	Pendant left 67·0°F.	+5·3 +5·9 +5·0 +2·8 +3·1	+4·4	0·9 1·5 0·6 1·6 1·3	1·18
17–22	Period IV 42°F.	Dial up 42·3°F.	Intermediate Day. −1·3 −3·2 −1·9 −2·4 −2·1	−2·2	0·9 1·0 0·3 0·2 0·1	0·50
23–28	Period V 67°F.	Dial up 66·8°F.	Intermediate Day. +2·9 +2·6 +3·0 +3·7 +2·5	+2·9	0·0 0·3 0·1 0·8 0·4	0·32
29–34	Period VI 92°F.	Dial up 92·2°F.	Intermediate Day. +2·6 +4·5 +4·2 +3·0 +1·9	+3·2	0·6 1·3 1·0 0·2 1·3	0·88

+ signifies gaining; − losing.

EXAMPLE OF THE DAILY PERFORMANCE OF A WATCH
OBTAINING 60 MARKS IN THE CLASS A TEST
continued.

Days of Test.	Period and Nominal Temperature.	Position and Mean Temperature of Watch.	Daily Rate. (seconds per day).	Mean Rate for Period (seconds per day)	Daily Variation from Mean Rate (seconds per day).	Mean Variation of Rate for Period (seconds per day).
				Intermediate Day.		
35–40	Period VII 67°F.	*Dial down* 66·9°F.	−0·9 −1·0 −3·2 −3·8 −4·5	2·7	1·8 1·7 0·5 1·1 1·8	1·38
40–45	Period VIII 67°F.	*Pendant up* 66·8°F.	+0·5 +4·5 +4·1 +4·3 +4·9	+3·7	3·2 0·8 0·4 0·6 1·2	1·24

+ signifies gaining; − losing.

SUMMARY OF FINAL RESULTS:
Grand mean variation of rate ..   ..   *a* = 0·95 secs. per day.
Mean change of rate with change of position *b* = 2·93 secs. per day.
Mean change of rate per 1°F. ..   ..   *c* = 0·139 secs. per day.

MARKS AWARDED:
In respect of consistency of daily rate ..   ..   21·0
In respect of constancy of rate with change of position   ..   28·3
In respect of temperature compensation   ..   ..   ..   10·7
                                                                   ————
                                          Total ..   ..   60·0

EXAMPLE OF THE DAILY PERFORMANCE OF A WATCH
OBTAINING 80 MARKS IN THE CLASS A TEST

Days of Test.	Period and Nominal Temperature.	Position and Mean Temperature of Watch.	Daily Rate (seconds per day).	Mean Rate for Period (seconds per day).	Daily Variation from Mean Rate (secs per day).	Mean Variation of Rate for Period (seconds per day).
1–6	Period I 67°F.	*Pendant up* 67·0°F.	−3·9 −4·3 −3·9 −4·3 −4·1	−4·1	0·2 0·2 0·2 0·2 0·0	0·16

+ signifies gaining;   − losing.

EXAMPLE OF THE DAILY PERFORMANCE OF A WATCH
OBTAINING 8c MARKS IN THE CLASS A TEST
continued,

Days of Test.	Period and Nominal Temperature.	Position and Mean Temperature of Watch.	Daily Rate (seconds per day).	Mean Rate for Period (seconds per day).	Daily Variation from Mean Rate (seconds per day).	Mean Variation of Rate for Period (seconds per day).
6–11	Period II 67°F.	Pendant right 67·2°F.	−3·8 −4·2 −4·4 −4·9 −5·0	−4·5	0·7 0·3 0·1 0·4 0·5	0·40
11–16	Period III 67°F.	Pendant left 67·1°F.	+2·6 +2·2 +2·0 +2·0 +1·8	+2·1	0·5 0·1 0·1 0·1 0·3	0·22
17–22	Period IV 42°F.	Dial up 41·6°F.	Intermediate Day. +1·1 0·0 −0·5 −0·6 −0·7	−0·1	1·2 0·1 0·4 0·5 0·6	0·56
23–28	Period V 67°F.	Dial up 66·8°F.	Intermediate Day. −2·0 −3·1 −3·7 −3·5 2·6	−3·0	1·0 0·1 0·7 0·5 0·4	0.54
29–34	Period VI 92°F.	Dial up 92·0°F.	Intermediate Day. −1·0 −0·4 +0·2 0·0 −0·2	−0·3	0·7 0·1 0·5 0·3 0·1	0·34
35–40	Period VII 67°F.	Dial down 67·1°F.	Intermediate Day. −2·5 −1·0 −1·6 −1·6 −0·3	−1·3	1·2 0·3 0·5 0·3 1·6	0·78

+ signifies gaining; − losing.

EXAMPLE OF THE DAILY PERFORMANCE OF A WATCH
OBTAINING 80 MARKS IN THE CLASS A TEST
continued.

Days of Test.	Period and Nominal Temperature.	Position and Mean Temperature of Watch.	Daily Rate (seconds per day).	Mean Rate for Period (seconds per day).	Daily Variation from Mean Rate (seconds per day).	Mean Variation of Rate for Period (seconds per day).
40–45	Period VIII 67°F.	*Pendant up* 67·4°F.	—2·4 —2·2 —1·9 —2·8 —2·6	—2·4	0·0 0·2 0·5 0·4 0·2	0.26

+ signifies gaining; — losing.

SUMMARY OF FINAL RESULTS:
Grand mean variation of rate   ..   .. $a = 0·41$ secs. per day.
Mean change of rate with change of position $b = 1·73$ secs. per day.
Mean change of rate per 1°F.   ..   .. $c = 0·073$ secs. per day

MARKS AWARDED:
In respect of consistency of daily rate ..   ..   31·8
In respect of constancy of rate with change of position   ..   33·1
In respect of temperature compensation   ..   ..   ..   15·1
                                                                ———
                                        Total ..   ..   80·0
                                                                ———

EXAMPLE OF THE DAILY PERFORMANCE OF A WATCH
OBTAINING 95 MARKS IN THE CLASS A TEST

Days of Test.	Period and Nominal Temperature.	Position and Mean Temperature of Watch.	Daily Rate. (seconds per day).	Mean Rate for Period (seconds per day).	Daily Variation from Mean Rate (seconds per day).	Mean Variation of Rate for Period (seconds per day).
1–6	Period I 67°F.	*Pendant up* 66·6°F.	—0·2 —0·1 —0·2 —0·1 —0·2	—0·2	0·0 0·1 0·0 0·1 0·0	0·04
6–11	Period II 67°F.	*Pendant right* 66·9°F	—1·4 —1·5 —1·3 —1·3 —1·2	—1·3	0·1 0·2 0·0 0·0 0·1	0·08
11–16	Period III 67°F.	*Pendant left* 67·0°F.	—1·1 —1·2 —1·1 —1·1 —1·3	—1·2	0·1 0·0 0·1 0·1 0·1	0·08

+ signifies gaining; — losing.

EXAMPLE OF THE DAILY PERFORMANCE OF A WATCH
OBTAINING 95 MARKS IN THE CLASS A TEST
continued.

Days of Test.	Period and Nominal Temperature.	Position and Mean Temperature of Watch.	Daily Rate (seconds per day).	Mean Rate for Period (seconds per day).	Daily Variation from Mean Rate (secs per day).	Mean Variation of Rate for Period (seconds per day).
			Intermediate Day.			
17–22	Period IV 42°F.	Dial up 42·4°F.	−1·2		0·1	
			−1·3		0·0	
			−1·3	−1·3	0·0	0·04
			−1·3		0·0	
			−1·2		0·1	
			Intermediate Day.			
23–28	Period V 67°F.	Dial up 66·6°F.	−1·9		0·1	
			−2·0		0·0	
			−2·0	−2·0	0·0	0·02
			−2·0		0·0	
			−2·0		0·0	
			Intermediate Day.			
29–34	Period VI 92°F.	Dial up 92·3°F.	−2·9		0·3	
			−2·9		0·3	
			−2·4	−2·6	0·2	0·26
			−2·4		0·2	
			−2·3		0·3	
			Intermediate Day.			
35–40	Period VII 67°F.	Dial down 66·8°F.	−0·9		0·2	
			−1·1		0·0	
			−1·0	−1·1	0·1	0·08
			−1·1		0·0	
			−1·2		0·1	
40–45	Period VIII. 67°F	Pendant up 67·0°F.	−0·6		0·1	
			−0·7		0·0	
			−0·7	−0·7	0·0	0·04
			−0·7		0·0	
			−0·8		0·1	

+ signifies gaining; − losing.

SUMMARY OF FINAL RESULTS:
Grand Mean variation of rate .. .. $a = 0·08$ secs. per day.
Mean change of rate with change of position $b = 0·42$ secs. per day.
Mean change of rate per 1°F. .. .. $c = 0·026$ secs. per day.

MARKS AWARDED:
In respect of consistency of daily rate .. .. 38·4
In respect of constancy of rate with change of position .. 38·3
In respect of temperature compensation .. .. .. 18·3
_____
Total .. .. 95·0

Total Marks.—The total marks awarded are therefore calculated from the formula :

$$\left(40 - \frac{a}{2} \times 40\right) + \left(40 - 4b\right) + \left(20 - \frac{c}{0 \cdot 3} \times 20\right)$$

i.e., $40\left(1 - \frac{a}{2}\right) + 40\left(1 - \frac{b}{10}\right) + 20\left(1 - \frac{c}{0 \cdot 3}\right)$

where a, b and c are defined above.

In the example, the marks awarded are:

In respect of consistency of daily rate ..	31·8
In respect of constancy of rate with change of position	33·1
In respect of constancy of rate with change of temperature	15·1
Grand total number of marks awarded	80·0

Examples of Performances of Class A Watches.—The examples given on pages 145, 146 and 148 illustrate the daily performance which may be expected from Class A watches obtaining 60, 80, and 95 marks respectively. In practice a watch which satisfies all the Class A tolerances would rarely obtain a total of less than 50 marks.

CHAPTER XXI

BRITISH HALL-MARKS

THE story of British hall-marks is a very necessary part of the education of the watchmaker. He will often be called upon to solve some question of date, style or maker by his client.

You will experience a real interest in this subject when you can say without hesitation which are the marks of London, Birmingham, Sheffield, Chester, Newcastle, Exeter, York, Norwich, Edinburgh, Glasgow, and by no means least, which are the marks of Ireland as represented by Dublin.

The Protection of the Hall-Mark.—At the commencement of the thirteenth century it was necessary to restrain by means of an ordinance the fraudulent use of more than the proper quantity of alloy in the manufacture of gold and silver ware, and to protect the public against the fraudulent use of inferior metal by the dishonest worker, and a little later it was found necessary to embody this principle in a law.

In 1300 it was decreed that no gold or silver ware should be sold until it had been assayed by a duly authorised person.

This law ordained that the mark of quality should be a leopard's head, and that wardens of the craft might visit the goldsmiths and silversmiths, search their stock, and anything found of less than the required quality was forfeited to the King.

Here is another interesting point—no goldsmith, silversmith or jeweller was allowed to set any stone in gold unless it was a natural one. Fortunately, or unfortunately, this law is not enforced to-day.

It was ordained that every goldsmith dwelling in the towns of England should be ordered to come to London "to be ascertained of his touch". There was thus a great army of craftsmen throughout the country who made beautiful silver, and who kept its quality. Although there was no convenient place where their goods could be stamped they identified their work first with a mark containing some reference to the arms of the town in which they practised, and secondly, with their own initials or monograms.

Craftsmen in Remote Towns.—Craftsmen working in remote

towns and villages of Cornwall, Devonshire, and other counties, found it very inconvenient, by reason of time, distance and risk, to send their work to the nearest hall to be marked, and that is why so many hundreds of provincial marks have puzzled the antiquary for many years. It was Chaffers and Cripps who led to the more complete investigation by Sir Charles Jackson, and later by De Castro.

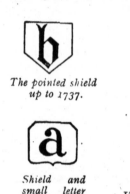

The pointed shield up to 1737.

Indented shield 1737-55.

Shield and black letter 1856-76.

Shield   and small   letter 1776-96.

Styles of London shields and letters.
1796-1816.   1816-36.   1836-56.

Leopard without crown 1821.

The King's head facing right, 1786.

The King's head facing left, 1789.

Old Chester mark.

Fig. 146.—Date letters.

It is still the law that no goldsmith or jeweller in the City of London should sell anything wrought of silver unless it is marked with a leopard's head, and that all articles imported should be marked in the same way as those made here. This explains why you find on an article a series of foreign marks, either Dutch, French or German, together with specially distinctive marks showing that these things are of foreign manufacture. Unless these articles are more than 100 years old they may not be sold without being sent to be assayed and marked.

Forgery.—The marks were further protected against forgery by a very severe penalty for counterfeiting the mark of another die, transposing the mark from one article of gold or silver to another, or the possession of a forged die or any article bearing the mark of a forged die or a transposed mark.

This is a very important law and one which many jewellers have unwittingly broken. There have been cases where the London Assay Office has searched stocks in London, within the last few years, for articles bearing these unlawful marks.

The necessity for this drastic action has been brought about by unscrupulous people who have used a small piece of silver with an old mark to incorporate it with a larger and more important piece, and constant watchfulness on the part of the wardens has been necessary during the years that marks have been compulsory.

The National Association of Goldsmiths was primarily formed with the object of resisting any attempt to interfere with the law of hall-marking, as there have been many attempts to restrict its power and to reduce quality.

This watchfulness has resulted in a series of marks being used by the hall which we call "hall marks", and we find that the British standard of plate, as represented by those marks, receives recognition in every country.

It is interesting to note that nearly all Continental countries have had their own system of hall-marks for many years, notably Holland, France, and Russia, whilst other countries have well-defined, guaranteed quality marks emanating from many of their provincial cities.

Now this country—especially London—possesses so clear a series of authenticated marks that it has become an easy matter to distinguish the very year in which they were placed, with very few exceptions, from 1478.

To place a particular mark to a particular date is quite an easy matter—one in fact which you can memorise without difficulty if certain quite easy references are borne in mind.

Memorising London Marks.—The London date letters are in a series of 20, omitting the letters J, W, X, Y and Z. This makes it very easy to memorise, because although the earlier lettering from the year 1478 commences with a different letter every 20 years, in 1696, 1716, etc.—every 20—the cycle is repeated.

The letter A thus represents the year 1716, and so on, in cycles of 20 years, and it therefore follows that if one memorises

Lion passant
London mark

Britannia
mark.

London

Birmingham

Sheffield.

Chester.

Edinburgh.

Glasgow.

Dublin.

Norwich.

Exeter.

York.

Newcastle.

Fig. 147.—
British hall-marks.

Norwich

the following letters, A, F, L, Q and V, each of these letters represent a 5-year period, say 1716 for A, 1721 for F, 1726 for L, 1731 for Q, and 1735 for the last letter V. In all the cycles these letters recur at exactly the same dates, and here you have the first of the secrets of the successful antique dealer who must recognise every date.

The second point to memorise is that all letters from the year 1559 are contained in a shield, and that these shields do not vary from the earliest period until 1737, the shield being of the Saxon type with a straight top, straight sides and a straight point. (Before this date the shield followed the shape of the letter.)

1737 is an important date to remember, and for the rest of this cycle, that is, from 1737 to 1755, the shield is indented at the sides. No other shield has this peculiar indentation and the cycle letters after this period are contained in a straight side shield with a curved point.

The cycle letters commencing with the year 1776 are contained in a similar shield, but the letters are in small black letter characters.

Duty Mark 1784-1890.—There is another important date to bear in mind in connection with this cycle—the year 1784 with the letter I or K, for at this time a duty mark of the King's head was introduced, and all series of marks afterwards included the King's or Queen's head until the year 1890, so that now one has 5 distinct and easily memorised points to bear in mind:

1. All the letters are contained in Saxon shields until the year 1737.
2. From 1696 the letters A, F, Q, L and V divided the cycles into 5-year periods, so that whenever you see the letter L you will know that this is 10 years after, i.e. 1716 or 1736, etc.
3. Wherever you see indented sides to the shield the piece belongs to a cycle commencing in 1736-1737.
4. Wherever you see old English letters without the head of the King it must be before the year 1776.
5. Wherever you see the King's head the date must have been after 1784.

With these points borne well in mind it is perfectly easy to trace any particular mark.

CHAPTER XXII

A WATCH DE-MAGNETISER

THE apparatus consists essentially of a magnetometer, that is, a sensitive magnetic compass, mounted on one end of a strip of wood, on the other end of which the solenoid is fixed. The actual woodwork will be left to the individual, but the important measurements are indicated here.

Obtain a piece of clock-spring, $\frac{1}{16}$ in. thick, and from it cut the magnet $\frac{3}{4} \times \frac{1}{2}$ in., soften by heating to redness and allowing to cool slowly, drill a $\frac{1}{8}$ in. hole in the exact centre, file off any burrs, and re-harden; to do this, heat to redness and immediately plunge into cold water. Wrap the steel with several layers of No. 36 insulated wire and connect to a 2-volt cell; if the current is too high, put a lamp or other suitable resistance in series; after 10 minutes the spring should be a strong magnet capable of lifting several pins.

The bearing for the needle is made from $\frac{1}{8}$ in. inside diameter glass tubing in the following way: take a length of tubing, say 3 or 4 in., and soften the centre in a bunsen flame, draw out to form a slightly constricted portion, and cut at A (see Fig. 148), which gives full details for making the bearing. Seal the constricted end of one tube, and to prevent the glass from becoming too thick and forming unevenly, blow gently down the tube. Cut the sealed end off the tube $\frac{1}{4}$ in. from the tip at B as shown. To cut tubing, mark round the glass with a fine triangular file, and then pull the pieces apart; a better grip may be obtained by holding the tube in a cloth.

The Bearing.—This must be a push-fit into the spring, and should project about $\frac{1}{8}$ in. on either side. The pointer for the instrument is about 3 in. long, and is cut from sheet aluminium about $\frac{1}{64}$ in. thick, as shown in Fig. 148 and the sketch of the completed instrument. The ends of the aluminium are bent at right-angles so as to give a knife-edged pointer. The pointer and magnet are both cemented to the bearing in the same operation, using some commercial glue or sealing wax; Allow to set quite hard before balancing. The instrument case is made about 4 in. square and 1 in. deep, inside measurements; the scale is a square of white card fitting tightly inside the box, resting on small blocks, with a centre hole 2 in. in diameter,

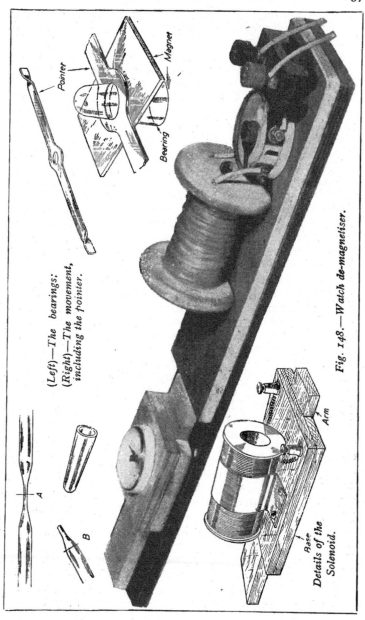

Pointer

Magnet

Bearing

(Left)—The bearings:
(Right)—The movement, including the pointer.

A

B

Arm

Base
Details of the Solenoid.

Fig. 148.—Watch de-magnetiser.

thus the pointer projects 2 in. at each end over the scale; the circle should be graduated in degrees. The box must be fitted with a glass lid. The magnet is suspended on a fine sewing needle that is stuck into a block of soft wood in the bottom of the box; the needle should be of such a height that it supports the pointer $\frac{1}{8}$ in. above the scale and in the exact centre of the box; balance the movement by grinding the magnet or filing the aluminium; when finished the pointer should lie east and west irrespective of the box position. Before the needle is finally mounted, fix a strip of wood, measuring $1 \times \frac{1}{2}$ in., to the bottom of the box, so that it is at right-angles to the magnetic meridian. The strip should be marked off from the centre of the box in inches or centimetres which shows a view of the completed instrument.

The Shape of the Solenoid.—This may be varied to suit individual requirements, but the most useful type is shown here. Make a bobbin from thin sheet brass with a centre hole of $\frac{1}{2}$ in., and end flanges 1 in. in diameter and length about $2\frac{1}{2}$ in.

Wind it to its maximum capacity with No. 26 D.C.C., observing the usual precautions. The bobbin is mounted on a suitable base that will slide along the wooden arm, and the ends are connected to two brass terminals. Fig. 148 gives a side view of the coil. In this work use only brass nails and screws; do not use any iron.

To use the apparatus set it up with the arm lying east and west, and connect the coil in series with a 2-volt cell and a variable resistance; a filament resistance will be ideal. Place the coil at the end of the arm and switch on; observe a deflection that increases as the current is increased, or as the coil is moved along the arm; note the increase in deflection when a piece of iron is placed in the coil. A small watch or similar piece of apparatus may be de-magnetised by placing at the end of the coil; larger coils will be required for larger instruments; it is not necessary for the instrument to fit inside the solenoid, provided that it is placed as near to it as possible. To de-magnetise, say, a piece of steel, place it in the coil and observe the deflection, say west; connect up the battery with the steel removed so as to make the needle move in the opposite direction, east; replace the steel and adjust the current and position of the solenoid until the needle is at zero. Switch off, and most probably, the pointer will return to a slightly west position, depending on the type of steel; switch on again and adjust until the needle is a few degrees east, repeat until the needle stays at zero when the current is switched off. The lagging effect is known briefly as hysteresis. To compare the strength of two bar magnets, place them at the same distance, measured from the centre of the magnet, along the arm, and observe the deflection; this is proportional to the strength of the magnets; thus, if one magnet gives twice the deflection of another, we may say, roughly, that one is twice as strong as the other, or one will lift twice as much as the other.

For Accurate Work.—Experiments on samples of iron and steel may be carried out quite simply, but for accurate work two exactly similar solenoids are required and placed at opposite sides of the magnetometer, so that when the current is switched on, the needle remains stationary. They are connected in series with the same battery, and if necessary, their positions altered, until the needle is at zero; thus, when a piece of iron is placed in one solenoid it is the magnetism passing through the iron that affects the needle and not the coils.

Magnetic Strengths.—The strength of an electro-magnet is dependent upon the "ampere-turns"; that is to say, the product of turns and current flowing, so that this feature may be borne in mind if for any reason it is desired to make a modification of the instrument which is described. If small batteries are to be employed it will obviously be desirable to restrict the current passed by the coil, and to obtain a high degree of magnetism with a small pole, it will in that case be necessary to increase the number of turns of wire. This could only be done by using a thinner wire, and, provided that the gauge is chosen with the current—carrying capacity in view, this should not be difficult. When dealing with very small bodies it may be found desirable, in fact preferable, to reduce the current passed by the coil. Whilst a lamp in series will be found quite a simple means of effecting this current reduction, a much better plan for serious work would be to fit a variable resistance in one battery lead. This may then be calibrated (if desired) so that various pre-determined settings may be obtained.

USEFUL TABLES
Waltham Watch Screw Taps

No. of Tap	No. of threads to an inch	Diameter of Thread on Screws		Diameter of Drill	
		In inches	In milli- metres	In inches	In milli- metres
I	110	0·05906	1·50	0·05197	1·32
3	110	0·04724	1·20	0·04016	1·02
5	120	0·04331	1·10	0·03741	0·95
7	140	0·03937	1·00	0·03347	0·85
9	160	0·03661	0·93	0·02796	0·71
11	170	0·05276	1·34	0·04803	1·22
13	180	0·03937	1·00	0·03347	0·85
15	180	0·03268	0·83	0·02796	0·71
17	200	0·02560	0·65	0·02126	0·54
19	220	0·02166	0·55	0·01772	0·45
21	240	0·01772	0·45	0·01339	0·34
23	254	0·01379	0·35	0·01064	0·27

Pendant Taps

Size	Diameter of Tap		Threads per inch	Diameter of Drill	
	Inches	Millimetres		Inches	Millimetres
18	·236	5·90	50	·211	5·28
16	·200	5·00	60	·180	4·50
12-6	·176	4·40	66	·158	3·95
0	·156	3·90	66	·138	3·45
5/0	·128	3·20	80	·114	2·85
10/0	·103	2·58	90	·086	2·15

Crown Taps

Size	Diameter of Tap		Threads per inch	Diameter of Drill	
	Inches	Millimetres		Inches	Millimetres
18	·091	2·28	60	·071	1·78
16	·077	1·93	72	063	1·58
12-6-0	·061	1·53	80	·048	1·20
5/0-10/0	·048	1·20	110	·038	0·95

Watchmakers' Measurements

Showing the comparative values of the standards of measurements commonly used by watchmakers.

One douzième = 0·0074 inch
One millimetre = 0·03937 inch
One ligne = 0·0888 inch
One ligne = 2·256 millimetres

The Elgin Watch Company has two gauges, one known as the "upright", the other as the "fine".

$$\text{One degree "upright" gauge} = \frac{1}{500} \text{ or } 0·002 \text{ inch}$$

$$\text{One degree "fine" gauge} = \frac{1}{2500} \text{ or } 0·0004 \text{ inch}$$

Table of Jewel-Setting Diameters

Showing their sizes in thousandths of an inch and equivalent diameters in millimetres

Inches	Millimetres	Inches	Millimetres	Inches	Millimetres
·054	1·37	·088	2·23	·126	3·20
·060	1·52	·092	2·33	·140	3·55
·070	1·78	·096	2·43	·144	3·65
·076	1·93	·106	2·69	·156	3·96
·080	2·03	·116	2·94	·160	4·06
·084	2·13	·122	3·09	·170	4·31
·086	2·18				

Thickness of Pallet Stones

In thousandths of an inch and equivalent thickness in millimetres.

	Inches	Millimetres
18 and 16 Old Style (thick)	0·0168	= 0·4267
18 and 16 New Style (thin)	0·0148	= 0·3759
6 Old Style (thick)	0·0146	= 0·3708
6 New Style (thin)	0·0128	= 0·3251

Elgin Watch Screw Taps

Diameter of Tap		Threads per Inch	Diameter of Drill	
Inches	Millimetres		Inches	Millimetres
·0132	·33	360	·0112	·28
·0148	·37	320	·0120	·30
·0168	·42	260	·0132	·33
·0208	·52	220	·0168	·42
·0228	·57	260	·0188	·47
·0248	·62	220	·0200	·50
·0268	·67	180	·0220	·55
·0288	·72	220	·0248	·62
·0308	·77	180	·0248	·62
·0308	·77	220	·0268	·67
·0368	·92	140	·0280	·70
·0368	·92	220	·0268	·67
·0408	1·02	120L	·0300	·75
·0408	1·02	200	·0348	·87
·0428	1·07	120	·0328	·82
·0448	1·12	110	·0340	·85
·0468	1·17	110	·0348	·87
·0488	1·22	140	·0400	1·00
·0488	1·22	200	·0436	1·09
·0508	1·27	110L	·0388	·97
·0548	1·37	180	·0488	1·22
·0608	1·52	110	·0488	1·22
·0608	1·52	110L	·0488	1·22
·0708	1·77	180L	·0648	1·62
·0768	1·92	110L	·0708	1·77
·0772	1·93	80L	·0612	1·53
·0892	2·23	80L	·0712	1·78

INDEX TO ADVERTISERS

Lightning Source UK Ltd.
Milton Keynes UK
UKOW01f0700060318
318970UK00001BA/61/P